28

D0743446

LIVING LIFE
AFTER DIVORCE &
WIDOWHOOD:

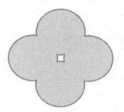

Financial Planning, Skills, and Strategies for When the Unthinkable Happens

By Maurcia DeLean Houck

332.0240086 HOUCK 2010

Houck, Maurcia DeLean.

Living life after divorce &
  widowhood

Library Resource Center
Renton Technical College
3000 N.E. 4th St.
Renton, WA 98056

LIVING LIFE AFTER DIVORCE & WIDOWHOOD: FINANCIAL PLANNING, SKILLS, AND STRATEGIES FOR WHEN THE UNTHINKABLE HAPPENS

Copyright © 2010 Atlantic Publishing Group, Inc.
1405 SW 6th Avenue • Ocala, Florida 34471 • Phone 800-814-1132 • Fax 352-622-1875
Web site: www.atlantic-pub.com • E-mail: sales@atlantic-pub.com
SAN Number: 268-1250

No part of this publication may be reproduced, stored in a retrieval system, or transmitted in any form or by any means, electronic, mechanical, photocopying, recording, scanning, or otherwise, except as permitted under Section 107 or 108 of the 1976 United States Copyright Act, without the prior written permission of the Publisher. Requests to the Publisher for permission should be sent to Atlantic Publishing Group, Inc., 1405 SW 6th Avenue, Ocala, Florida 34471.

Library of Congress Cataloging-in-Publication Data

Houck, Maurcia DeLean.
 Living life after divorce & widowhood : financial planning, skills, and strategies for when the unthinkable happens / Maurcia DeLean Houcká.
   p. cm.
Includes bibliographical references and index.
ISBN-13: 978-1-60138-289-4 (alk. paper)
ISBN-10: 1-60138-289-8 (alk. paper)
1. Widows--United States--Finance, Personal. 2. Widowers--United States--Finance, Personal. 3. Divorced women--United States--Finance, Personal. 4. Divorced men--United States--Finance, Personal. 5. Estate planning--United States. I. Title.
 HG179.H599 2009
 332.0240086'53--dc22
                2009034576

LIMIT OF LIABILITY/DISCLAIMER OF WARRANTY: The publisher and the author make no representations or warranties with respect to the accuracy or completeness of the contents of this work and specifically disclaim all warranties, including without limitation warranties of fitness for a particular purpose. No warranty may be created or extended by sales or promotional materials. The advice and strategies contained herein may not be suitable for every situation. This work is sold with the understanding that the publisher is not engaged in rendering legal, accounting, or other professional services. If professional assistance is required, the services of a competent professional should be sought. Neither the publisher nor the author shall be liable for damages arising herefrom. The fact that an organization or Web site is referred to in this work as a citation and/or a potential source of further information does not mean that the author or the publisher endorses the information the organization or Web site may provide or recommendations it may make. Further, readers should be aware that Internet Web sites listed in this work may have changed or disappeared between when this work was written and when it is read.

Printed in the United States

PROJECT MANAGER: Kim Fulscher • kfulscher@atlantic-pub.com
ASSISTANT EDITOR: Angela Pham • apham@atlantic-pub.com
INTERIOR DESIGN: Holly Marie Gibbs • hgibbs@atlantic-pub.com
INTERIOR LAYOUT: T.L. Price • design@tlpricefreelance.com
COVER DESIGN: Meg Buchner • meg@megbuchner.com
JACKET DESIGN: Jackie Miller • sullmill@charter.net

Printed on Recycled Paper

We recently lost our beloved pet "Bear," who was not only our best and dearest friend but also the "Vice President of Sunshine" here at Atlantic Publishing. He did not receive a salary but worked tirelessly 24 hours a day to please his parents. Bear was a rescue dog that turned around and showered myself, my wife, Sherri, his grandparents Jean, Bob, and Nancy, and every person and animal he met (maybe not rabbits) with friendship and love. He made a lot of people smile every day.

We wanted you to know that a portion of the profits of this book will be donated to The Humane Society of the United States. *–Douglas & Sherri Brown*

The human-animal bond is as old as human history. We cherish our animal companions for their unconditional affection and acceptance. We feel a thrill when we glimpse wild creatures in their natural habitat or in our own backyard.

Unfortunately, the human-animal bond has at times been weakened. Humans have exploited some animal species to the point of extinction.

The Humane Society of the United States makes a difference in the lives of animals here at home and worldwide. The HSUS is dedicated to creating a world where our relationship with animals is guided by compassion. We seek a truly humane society in which animals are respected for their intrinsic value, and where the human-animal bond is strong.

Want to help animals? We have plenty of suggestions. Adopt a pet from a local shelter, join The Humane Society and be a part of our work to help companion animals and wildlife. You will be funding our educational, legislative, investigative and outreach projects in the U.S. and across the globe.

Or perhaps you'd like to make a memorial donation in honor of a pet, friend or relative? You can through our Kindred Spirits program. And if you'd like to contribute in a more structured way, our Planned Giving Office has suggestions about estate planning, annuities, and even gifts of stock that avoid capital gains taxes.

Maybe you have land that you would like to preserve as a lasting habitat for wildlife. Our Wildlife Land Trust can help you. Perhaps the land you want to share is a backyard—that's enough. Our Urban Wildlife Sanctuary Program will show you how to create a habitat for your wild neighbors.

So you see, it's easy to help animals. And The HSUS is here to help.

THE HUMANE SOCIETY
OF THE UNITED STATES.

2100 L Street NW • Washington, DC 20037 • 202-452-1100
www.hsus.org

TABLE OF CONTENTS

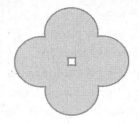

Chapter 2: What's Ahead — How the Death of Your Spouse Will Affect Your Financial Future   33

Chapter 3: How to Safeguard Your Financial Future Before You File for Divorce   57

Chapter 10: Ask Uncle Sam – Understanding Your New Tax Reality   163

Chapter 11: Understanding Child Support and Alimony   173

PART III: Moving On — 189

Chapter 12: Dealing with Your Grief — 191

Chapter 13: Dealing with Life's Practicalities — 201

Chapter 14: Securing Your Child's Future   209

Chapter 15: The Return to Normal   ·   225

Library Resource Center
Renton Technical College
3000 N.E. 4th St.
Renton, WA 98056

FOREWORD

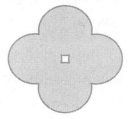

Financial Planning in Divorce and Widowhood

Divorce Financial Planning

In September 1969, Governor Ronald Reagan signed into law the California Family Law Act. This was the first "no-fault" divorce law in the United States. No-fault divorce rapidly spread to other states and quickly changed the focus of divorce from "fault" to "finance." Today, the only state that does not have a no-fault divorce statute is New York.

Although it has been about 40 years since the original legislation — and divorce in all states is now largely about money — incompatibilities have remained between the pre-existing divorce advocacy system and the need to find fair and workable outcomes. Because of this, it is not uncommon to see financial outcomes based on the fruits of strong advocacy rather than such factors as the needs and paying abilities of the parties and their pre-divorce standard of living. Unfortunately, children are often innocent victims of this process.

Over the past several years, there has been an increased application of alternative dispute resolution methods, such as mediation and interdisciplinary collaborative divorce to the divorce process. While not suitable in all situations, these methods frequently lead to better results, with less collateral damage. Furthermore, interdisciplinary collaborative divorce includes the use of financial specialists on the divorce team, who provide the useful financial input during the process.

In the mid-1980s, the field of divorce financial planning — a subspecialty of traditional financial planning — was born, and today, many divorce financial planners participate in litigated and mediated cases, as well as on collaborative divorce teams. The broad educational background of the financial planner is ideally suited for this type of work. And because planners have historically helped individuals achieve long-term financial goals, they have specialized training and skills that enable them to analyze financial issues in their long-term economic contexts. This has been extremely helpful for people going through divorce.

Whatever method people choose to resolve their divorce, they need to make important decisions as they proceed through the process. If they ultimately make bad decisions, they more than likely will have to live with the consequences of those decisions. Unfortunately, those consequences can potentially be financially or emotionally devastating, thus it is important that they get things right.

While it is essential to find the right professionals to work with or represent you during the process, it is also crucial to know that you — not your attorney, mediator, or financial planner — is ultimately responsible for the outcome of your divorce. Hiring the right people is obviously an important part of your job but, as in many other areas of life, knowledge in divorce is king. Whatever else you do, it is important to continuously educate yourself about the process, especially all of its financial intricacies.

Financial Planning and Widowhood

In divorce, widows and widowers are confronted with an immediate need to effectively manage myriad issues, many of which will be financial. Despite the emotional stress they will most assuredly be under, they will need to make important short- and long-term decisions with possible long-lasting effects. And it is important these decisions be made rationally and with a strong knowledge of the relevant facts and the financial consequences. If decisions are made without proper forethought, the financial and emotional effects can be devastating.

Typically, the financial planning process in widowhood begins with stabilization of the situation and attention to immediate needs. The next step usually involves collection and analysis of relevant financial data, including information about assets and liabilities, Social Security, life insurance, health insurance, and retirement benefits. In general, important decisions regarding financial issues should not be made until this process is complete. Because this task can sometimes appear overwhelming to the recent widow or widower, a financial planner is often helpful in identifying and collecting the necessary information and providing useful insights.

Proper financial planning can help widows and widowers reduce stress, stay focused, and take control over the important issues at hand, thus enabling them to begin the process of rebuilding their lives and enhancing their financial futures. Although they may often hire an attorney or financial planner to help them deal with certain issues, they are ultimately responsible for their own futures. Here, knowledge is king.

About the Book

Living Life After Divorce and Widowhood: Financial Planning Skills and Strategies for When the Unthinkable Happens is an excellent starting point for acquiring knowledge, tools, and resources useful in identifying, preparing for, and taking control over the often overlapping financial issues of divorce and widowhood. While not a substitute for professional advice, this book is easy to read, well-organized, and chock-full of useful information, to help you better understand your situation and find and learn how to work effectively with appropriate professionals. Going forward, it can get you started on the road to recovery and help you take positive and pro-active control of the rest of your life.

Carl M. Palatnik, Ph.D., CFP®, CDFA™
CERTIFIED FINANCIAL PLANNER™ practitioner
Certified Divorce Financial Analyst™
Founding President of the Association of Divorce Financial Planners
www.divorceandfinance.org
888-838-7773

INTRODUCTION

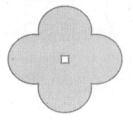

Life and marriage can take many twists and turns over the years — some widely anticipated, such as the birth of a child or the purchase of a dream home, and some unwanted and unanticipated, such as the death of a beloved spouse or a divorce.

Although different in many aspects, one thing is for certain when faced with either death or divorce: Your life will never be the same.

In addition to the emotional aspects that must be dealt with, facing either of these horrific events plays havoc on more than just your life as you know it — it can devastate your finances.

The financial fallout from an unexpected death or a divorce can leave you vulnerable for years to come. Add to that the dilemma of having to take control of your finances once again — not to mention relearning the single lifestyle — and you could be left struggling just to survive in the weeks or months following your entry into this new, solo world.

Living Life After Divorce and Widowhood is a practical guide designed to help you keep yourself afloat during this difficult transition. Within its pages, you will learn important strategies designed to not only help you better navigate the financial challenges you are bound to encounter, but also to come through them stronger and wiser than you ever thought possible.

Learning how to take care of your own finances can be scary, especially if you have always left that job up to your spouse. But, rest assured, you can do it — and this book is going to show you how.

In "Part I: Making Plans," the guide will help you plan for the worst by helping you to:

- Face the facts about your financial life
- Get yourself organized
- Be proactive when dealing with a terminally ill spouse
- Maneuver through the life insurance maze
- Seek help when dealing with a dissatisfied spouse
- Understand your rights and benefits in these situations

Once you have begun to see your situation for what it is, it is time for "Part II: Getting Your Financial Life in Order. "

Nobody wants to think about money at a time like this. Right now, you are likely feeling hurt, angry, and frightened. Those are all legitimate feelings, but the sooner you can dig into those important financial matters, the faster you will be able to take back control of your life (or at least some small segment of it), and the less havoc these financial matters will cause.

In "Part II: Getting Your Financial Life in Order," you will take a closer look at your finances, and you will learn some basic budgeting strategies to get you started on the road to financial freedom by explaining how to:

- Assess your bills
- Restructure your spending habits
- Create a livable budget

- Divide your assets equitably (in the case of a divorce)
- Manage your savings & retirement investments properly
- Understand the impact your singleness will have on your taxes
- Get the child or spousal support you need and deserve

Although it may be hard to believe right now, there is life after the loss of your spouse, whether it is by death or divorce. You can — and will — move on, when you are ready.

"Part III: Moving On" addresses the importance of making big changes in your life, which may include going back to work, getting your degree, or even pulling up roots and starting fresh somewhere else.

In addition to addressing these important personal changes, this section will also reveal more practical matters, such as changing your beneficiaries and power of attorney, saving for your child's future, and even how remarrying may once again disrupt your finances — and how to safeguard what you have built.

Ready for it or not, life has thrown you a curveball, and you are moving in a new direction. You can embrace this journey and learn from it, or you can let it beat you down. Do not let the financial obstacles ahead make you so fearful that you are not able to take that next big step into the unknown world of singleness. Let this book help you maneuver through the financial abyss that lies ahead to build a stronger financial life for yourself.

There are many decisions to be made in the days, weeks, and months to come. Make sure you are ready for them. Do not let your lack of financial savvy sabotage your efforts. A strong financial future lies ahead, and you are going to learn how to make the decisions necessary to make sure you get it.

PART 1

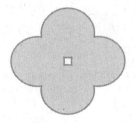

Making Plans

CHAPTER 1

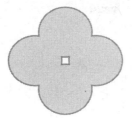

Taking the Lead to Prepare for the Worst

No one wants to consider that the worst can happen. Unfortunately, tragedy does strike: Spouses may die or become ill, or they simply announce one day that they are leaving. That does not mean your financial life has to be left in shambles — if you take the lead and prepare for the storm ahead.

Developing a Proactive Plan for the Terminally Ill

No one wants to face his or her mortality head-on, and you certainly do not want to plan the demise of someone you love. However, if you allow yourself to take the courageous step to prepare for your spouse's death, you could save your family from the problems that may wait.

When faced with the imminent death of your spouse, ask a faithful friend or family member to help you deal with the following tasks while you still have time to think each step through. Make the most logical — not emotional — decision you can for yourself and your family's future:

Step No. 1: Organize Your Important Papers

There are piles of paperwork involved in someone's death. Waiting until after you say goodbye to try and find everything you need, such as important insurance papers or retirement account information, is not only stressful; it can become a burden for those left behind. While your spouse is still well enough to know — and remember — where his or her most important documents are, gather the following together in one place:

- Last will and testament
- Living will
- Health care proxy
- Power of attorney
- Birth certificate
- Social Security number
- Life insurance documents
- Health insurance documents, including the policy numbers, benefits summary, and flexible benefits account. You may also want to contact your health insurance company now to see how long you and your dependents will be covered once the primary cardholder has passed.
- Passport
- Marriage certificate
- Mortgage papers or property deed
- Titles of all cars, trucks, boats, and recreation vehicles
- Tax returns for the last three to five years
- Investment savings reports
- Bank account information
- Loan statements
- Credit card statements
- Student loan statements
- Child custody agreements
- Armed forces service and discharge papers

- Credit, debit, and ATM cards, including balances, insurance coverage on cards, PIN numbers, and any other pertinent information you will need.

Step No. 2: Make a List of Important People to Be Contacted

Once you have gathered these basic documents, it is time to think about the people who will need to be notified of your spouse's death once it happens. The sheer volume of calls you will need to make may overwhelm you; these will be both personal and professional calls. By taking the time to make a list of people and their phone numbers now, you will make it easier on those willing to help you make them later. Some of the people you should list include:

- Close friends, family, and colleagues
- Spouse's estate executor
- Certified financial planner / accountant
- Lawyer
- Funeral director
- Physicians
- Work supervisor
- Pastor / church family
- Insurance agent
- Banker

Step No. 3: Plan for an Easier Financial Transition

In the event all of your ready cash is held in accounts bearing your spouse's name, you might find yourself unable to access the money you need to pay the bills for a few weeks following his or her death. Take some time now to open an account in your own name, and transfer utility monies there. Life insurance and Social Security benefits take time to be disbursed, and you will need cash available to live on in the meantime. A few other things you can do to make your financial transition from a married couple to a widowed single are to:

- Consolidate multiple bank accounts into one or two, but be sure that no single account contains more than $250,000. This amount is what the Federal Reserve will guarantee should the bank suddenly close its doors. On January 1, 2014, the amount will decrease to $100,000 for each depositor for all account categories. This does not include IRAs and other certain retirement accounts, which will remain at $250,000 for each depositor. Another item to consider: Consolidate accounts with multiple institutions into accounts with just one bank or credit union to make it easier to keep track of what accounts (and money) you have.

- Consolidate brokerage accounts.

- Put all jointly held accounts in the surviving spouse's name. This will eliminate the need to have your accounts placed in the person's estate and liquidated from there.

- Transfer vehicle and property ownership into the survivor's (or beneficiaries') name to avoid prolonged legal proceedings and paying inheritance taxes.

Step No. 4: Document All the Practical Stuff

It is amazing how many seemingly insignificant details our lives contain. Take a hard look at the dying spouse's personal and professional lives to see what details need to be taken care of after his or her death. Maybe the person has numerous magazine or newspaper subscriptions that will need to be canceled, or maybe he or she belongs to several professional organizations that charge hefty annual fees. Next, take the time to write down all the codes and passwords your spouse uses to access accounts, start the computer, turn off the security system, and perform other tasks. These are all the things you do not think about until it is too late to know the answers.

Step No. 5: Make Funeral Arrangements Now

For some, the thought of pre-planning a funeral seems morbid, while others find comfort in the thought of knowing they are able to give their spouse the funeral he or she wants and deserves. By pre-planning a funeral, you can save time and money after the death, be able to concentrate on more personal ways to make this memorial special to all involved, and ease the emotional distress that is bound to engulf survivors in the hours and days following a death.

When possible, speak with a local funeral director to get a better idea of what is involved, both practically and financially, following the death of a loved one. Even if you do not opt for a pre-planned funeral, you will still have the peace of mind of knowing what to expect so you are not caught by surprise later.

No matter how much time you take to prepare before the death of a terminally ill spouse, there are still many details that will go undone, and they will need to be taken care of at the worst possible time — immediately following your loss. However, by getting a handle on your family's finances and your spouse's important papers now, you will be left with less to deal with later.

Are You Ever Ready To Say Goodbye?

It does not matter whether you are 20, 30, 50 or 80: You are never truly ready to say goodbye to the one who promised to love and cherish you through the best and worst of life. But the worst can happen, and you will be forced to face it alone.

Despite this disheartening fact, there are things you can do now to prepare for the more mundane aspects of your life — including your finances — in order to free yourself emotionally to tackle the changes that lie ahead. Now, let us take a good look at how you can begin to prepare financially for your spouse's death.

Taking Care of Yourself While Caring for a Dying Spouse

When you are faced with the reality that your spouse is going to die, you may be tempted to make every aspect of your life revolve around his or her last days. While it is important to do everything you can to help your spouse through this transition, it is also important that you take some time to take care of yourself. There is a lot to do, including taking care of his or her medical and emotional needs and figuring out your finances before you are left alone. Now it is time to add one more thing to that list: taking care of your physical and emotional needs. If you do not, you may be left with nothing left to give either physically or emotionally when your spouse and the rest of the family need you most. Here are a few tips for taking time for you without feeling guilty:

- Do something that used to bring you pleasure, even if you do not feel like it right now. Work in the garden, engage in a hobby, or simply read a good book.

- Take time out. Now is the time to pamper yourself a little: Indulge in a bubble bath; listen to your favorite music; watch a movie; or take an afternoon and go to the spa.

- Eat a well-balanced diet and find time to exercise regularly. Do your best to get at least seven hours of sleep each night. Otherwise, you may deplete your body of what it needs to stay focused and healthy.

- Find something to laugh about. Laughter is often called the best medicine, so give yourself a good shot of humor to try and keep your spirits up during this difficult time.

- Write out your feelings. Don't keep it all bottled up inside. Maybe you cannot share your innermost feelings with anyone else right now, but you can write them down. Not only will it help you release your fears and anxiety, but it can help you gain a better perspective on your life right now.

- Stay in touch with other people in your life. Make sure to talk with someone at least once a day. They can help you keep things in perspective and give you an outlet for your thoughts and emotions.

- Join a support group. Even if you cannot leave your home, find a group online where you can interact with others going through the same situation you are.

- Lean on your church. There are people there who want to help out, so let them. Find someone to pray with you, listen to you, or maybe even sit with your spouse for an hour or so to give you a much-needed break. No one can go it alone for long. Be sure to get the support you need to get through this trying time.

Finding Good Hospice Care

Finding the right hospice program to handle your spouse's care in his or her last days can be daunting, but it does not have to be. There are plenty of resources available to help you get started. The first thing you must do is answer these simple questions, and then look for help in the resource guide listed below:

Question No. 1: What type of care am I looking for (in-home, facility, etc.)?

Question No. 2: What types of services will we need?

Question No. 3: What type of special training and staff needs do we want and need?

Question No. 4: What types of facilities/programs will our insurance cover?

Question No. 5: Is there a limitation on the time and services our insurance will cover?

Question No. 6: Do we have any special needs that must be addressed?

Local Resources

There are plenty of local resources to help you locate the type of program or facility you need including:

- Your doctor
- Your hospital discharge planner
- The local telephone book
- Local offices of the American Cancer Society, (**www.cancer.org**), an Agency on Aging, (**www.agingcarefl.org**), a local United Way chapter, (**www. liveunited.org**), the Visiting Nurse Association, (**www.vnaa.org**), or your place of worship.

State Resources

Your Department of Health or Social Services may be able to provide you with a listing of state certified hospice agencies and/or programs. The phone book is another great place to find the help you need. Often, special service organizations and/or agencies are listed in the colored pages right before the general listings.

National Resources

No matter what the problem, there seems to be a national organization that offers research, information, and other types of support. Hospice care is no different. Check out a few search engines on the Internet to find an organization that can put you in touch with an accredited agency in your area.

How Much Does Your Child Understand?

You know that your spouse is dying, leaving you with much to do to handle your own financial circumstances and grief. However, how much does your child really understand during this time?

According to most grief experts, children are more aware of what is happening than many of the adults around them give them credit for. This can be a negative ability, leaving them with unanswered questions and fears when those around them fail to consider what they are going through.

To better understand how much your children understand about your spouse's impending death, consider this:

- Children from birth to age 5 usually are unable to completely grasp the permanence of death and may ask continual questions as a coping mechanism.

- Children between the ages of 6 and 8 do understand the permanence of death, but may combine facts and perceptions to come up with a "new reality." Children in this age group need constant clarification to make sure they understand what has happened and give them plenty of opportunity to express their emotions.

- Children ages 9 to 12 are seekers, tending to cope with the realities of life by fixating on learning all of the facts. This may result in them researching the parent's cause of death and fixating on it for a period of time. While often unsettling to the adults in their life, it is a completely normal coping mechanism and should not be discouraged.

- Teenagers completely understand the permanence of death and often rebel with a lot of emotional outbursts or mood swings.

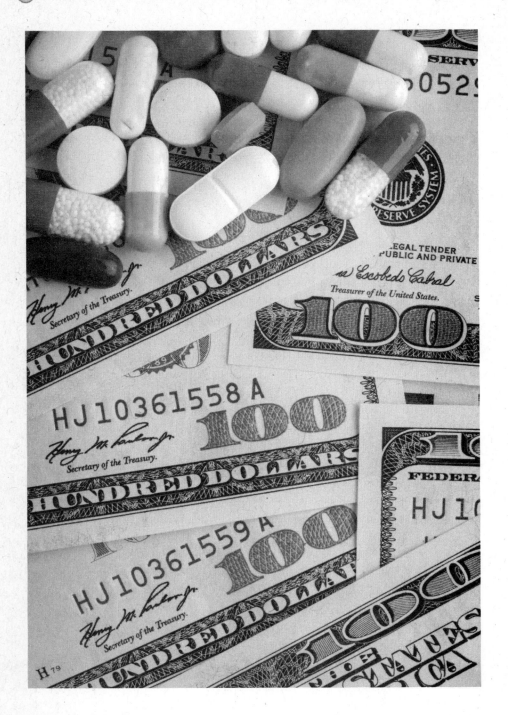

CHAPTER 2:

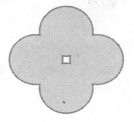

What's Ahead — How the Death of Your Spouse Will Affect Your Financial Future

Losing your spouse can be one of the most financially taxing experiences you will ever face. For some, the burden is lightened somewhat by life insurance benefits, while others must face the harsh realities of their family's financial state. Either way, your life — and your lifestyle — will change after your loved one's death.

That is why it is so important to take a close look at the main changes we have listed below that are likely to occur following the death of a spouse. While you recognize there will be many more decisions for you to make in the coming weeks and months, these are the three main things that must be addressed right away to ensure that your financial state does not disrupt your daily life more than it has to — at least for now.

Change No. 1: Your Income

Expect your income to change drastically following the death of your spouse, especially if that spouse was the family breadwinner. The first major difference you will see is the source of your income. Although you previously relied on your spouse's salary to pay the bills, you may now have to rely on Social Security benefits, which will likely be much less than you are used to. If you are lucky, life insurance payments or investment income can financially help.

What to do if your new income falls short of paying for your current lifestyle will be addressed in detail in Chapter 6. For now, you are going to concentrate on figuring out how much money you can depend on every month.

Social Security Benefits

Once called "widow's benefits," the U.S. Social Security Administration offers a portion of the deceased's Social Security benefits in the form of survivor benefits to the spouses and minor children of those who would have qualified for a monthly retirement check. Under certain circumstances, even a deceased's elderly parents may collect benefits — but only if the deceased supported them financially.

There are two types of Social Security benefits offered by the federal government:

1. A one-time lump sum of $255 to help pay for funeral costs

2. A monthly survivor benefit that is calculated by the retirement benefits the deceased would have qualified for at retirement age. This benefit runs between 70 and 100 percent of the projected retirement benefit, depending on who qualifies. Of course, there are maximums allowed by law. Most American workers receive an annual review of their benefits from the Social Security office that clearly states the death benefits allowed by the worker's family in the event of his or her death. Finding a copy of this benefit sheet will tell you

right away what your monthly benefits check will be. Otherwise, you will have to wait for the Social Security Administrative Office (**www.ssa.gov**) to calculate the benefit for you.

To qualify for either of these benefits, you will have to make a formal request and prove that you meet the qualifying standards. This includes making sure that the deceased spouse was indeed "insured" by the government. To qualify for benefits, a worker must be insured or must have worked enough hours during his or her adult life to wrack up enough "credits" for retirement savings. The younger you are, the fewer credits you need to be "insurable." Those individuals who did not earn enough credits may leave their survivors with no benefits at all.

The second qualifier is for the surviving family members themselves. To qualify for Social Security benefits, a survivor must:

- Have been married to the deceased for at least nine months prior to the death, unless it is caused by an accident or military duty

- Be a divorced spouse whose marriage lasted at least ten years

- Be the parent (or legal guardian) of the deceased's minor child

- Be at least 60 years of age, disabled, or caring for the deceased's child under the age of 16

- Be the natural, adopted, or stepchild (who was at least 50 percent dependent on the deceased's support), or a dependent grandchild, who is either under the age of 18, or who may have been disabled before the age of 22 and requires ongoing care.

- Be 62 years of age or older and the parent of the deceased, if you relied on at least 50 percent of your monthly support from the deceased

To learn more about the qualifying standards for collecting Social Security benefits for you and your children, call 1-800-772-1213 and request the Social Security Survivor Benefits booklet (publication #05-10084). Or, you can download it at **www.ssa.gov/pubs/10084.html.**

Collecting Social Security Benefits

The amount of money you will receive following your spouse's death depends largely on how much the person contributed during his or her working years. The more money contributed, the larger the death benefit.

With any type of government bureaucracy, filing for Social Security benefits can take time and tax your patience, so it is important to begin the process as soon as possible. When filing for benefits, you will need to gather plenty of information. Here is a rundown of the type of information and documents you may be required to present during the application and interview process:

- Social Security numbers: You must submit the Social Security numbers of all involved individuals — the deceased, yourself, and any minor children applying for benefits

- Your name and your spouse's name at birth, if different

- Birth certificates: This legal documentation will be required for survivors as well as the deceased

- Death certificate

- The deceased's last address

- Whether the deceased had already filed (or was receiving) any Social Security or Medicare benefits

- Whether the survivors have become disabled or unable to work during the last 14 months — and why

- Whether the deceased was unable to work during the last 14 months due to illness or injury — and why

- Military service reports: It is important to notify the Social Security Administration if the deceased was an active service person before 1968, as this could affect your benefits and pension monies owed. Discharge records may be required

- Employment history: Certain industries pay an additional annuity or pension. Be sure to list any work done by either you or the deceased in the railroad industry. Another thing to consider is Social Security benefits paid to other countries during work aboard. This may entitle you to benefits from that country also

- Marriage certificates: You will be required to produce not only your own marriage certificate, but the marriage certificates and divorce decrees from any marriages your deceased spouse may have had in the past

- Income and earnings: The amount of your spouse's earnings and your own during the three years preceding his or her death

- The names and Social Security numbers of any parents who may have relied on your spouse for support

- A date on which you would like your benefits to begin

Do not be intimidated by this list. There are agencies that can help you gather the information and documents you need, including the Social Security Administration.

> **TIP:**
>
> The Consumer Information Center (#526B, Pueblo, CO 81009) offers a great free guide called *Social Security: What Every Woman Should Know*, which covers everything from employment taxes and changes in marriage status to retirement. To order your free copy, simply write to the address listed above.

Life Insurance

In addition to collecting one-time or monthly Social Security benefits following your spouse's death, you may receive life insurance benefits as well. In most cases, life insurance provides the spouse and family the most benefits after a loved one's death.

If you are unsure whether your spouse had life insurance, there are several places for you to look to see whether a policy exists:

- The carrier that handles your other insurance needs.

- Your mortgage company. Many mortgage lenders offer inexpensive mortgage insurance policies that pay off your mortgage in the event of the mortgage holder's death.

- Your spouse's employer. Check with the human resources department at your spouse's place of employment. Many employers offer small policies ranging anywhere from $10,000 to twice the employee's salary as an added work benefit. The higher your spouse's position in the company, the better the chance that the company holds a policy on him or her for you. Depending on the types of jobs your spouse has had in the past, it may be a good idea to check with previous employers also, especially if he or she worked for someone else for a long period of time.

- The military. Depending on the type of military service offered, you may qualify for extra insurance or pension payments. Low-cost plans are also available, starting at $28 a year.

- Any organizations in which your spouse was an active member. Many social, professional, and union organizations offer group life insurance plans for their members. Be sure to see whether such a policy exists for your spouse.

- Your spouse's credit card accounts. Many banks and credit card companies these days offer accidental death coverage in the event of a cardholder's death. Because the premium is relatively small, many people opt for this limited coverage, with little thought to recording it in their important papers.

Once you figure out what kind of life insurance policy or policies are held on your spouse, you will need to research how the death benefits will ultimately be paid. The most common forms are:

1. Lump sum payments: This gives the beneficiary the entire benefit amount at one time

2. Specific income provision: This type of policy allows the life insurance carrier to distribute benefits in accordance to a pre-determined (and agreed upon) schedule.

3. Life income option: This gives the policy holder's survivor a monthly stipend until the person's own death. The amount is dependent on the policy's benefits and the survivor's age.

4. Interest income option. With this type of policy, the insurance company will pay the beneficiary the interest earned on the policy on an annual basis. Upon the death of the survivor, the actual death benefit will be paid to your children or other secondary beneficiary.

Making a Claim

When making a claim for life insurance benefits, you will be required to contact the agent, group, or insurance carrier for the proper forms. Group policies, such as those held by organizations and employers, are handled in-house. You will be able to obtain the necessary forms directly from them.

Filing a claim for a privately held policy may take more work, and paperwork, on your part. Contact the agent or company whose name appears on the policy. You will need a copy of the policy and/or the policy number to begin the claim process. In the event that you cannot locate a copy of the policy, or do not know which agent was used, you can contact the policy search division at The American Council of Life Insurers (**www.acli.com**) in Washington, D.C., for assistance. If there is a policy listed in the deceased's name, regardless of the carrier, they will find it and give you the information you need to submit your claim. This is a free service offered by the federal government.

Once you have the policy number in hand, contact the life insurance carrier and request a claim packet, which will describe the entire process and provide you with the forms necessary to file your claim.

Some important documents to begin gathering before your claims packet arrives include:

- Certified copy of your spouse's death certificate
- Insurance policy number
- Policy's face value
- Deceased's occupation on his or her last day of work
- Deceased's birth certificate, as well as your own
- Attending physician's statement
- Coroner's report, if applicable
- Police report, if applicable
- Beneficiary's legal name, address, and Social Security number

Employee Benefits

One thing many survivors fail to realize is they may be eligible for additional benefits from their loved one's current — or even past — employers. Some of the benefits you may find yourself qualified to receive include:

- Any unpaid salary
- Any unpaid sick days or vacation time
- Workers' compensation
- Disability payments
- Pensions
- 401(k) contributions
- Accrued bonus monies
- Flex benefits

Retirement Savings

The rules for disbursing retirement savings differ depending on the type of the account, the type of beneficiary you are (i.e., spouse, non-spouse, entity, or trust) and the age or ages of all beneficiaries. Check with a certified public accountant or financial planner for guidelines. Most IRAs and 401(k) plans require beneficiaries to begin taking required minimum distributions (RMD) from inherited IRAs at some point.

Veteran's Benefits

The Department of Veteran's Affairs (VA — their Web site can be visited at **www.va.gov**) offers a variety of death benefits to the survivors of our country's veterans. Although benefits vary depending on the type of service (wartime veterans are eligible for more), the amount of time served, and other variables, all veterans' survivors are eligible for some help.

For instance, the families of most veterans qualify for up to $2,000 in reimbursement for burial costs, a free headstone or marker, a burial flag, and, in some cases, burial in VA National Cemetery. You can also be buried at sea. Some may also qualify for a veteran's pension and, in some cases, may even qualify for help obtaining or paying for medical services for the surviving spouse and dependents.

There is no time limit in requesting these benefits, so if you were not aware of them at the time of your spouse's death, you can apply years later and receive the benefits due to you. To find out more about these and other benefits offered by the Veteran's Administrative Offices (VA), call 1-800- 827-1000 or visit your local office today.

Now that you have a clearer idea of the income you can expect after your spouse has died, look at some other changes you are likely to experience.

Change No. 2: Your Health Care

One of the biggest financial hurdles you may have to overcome following the death of your spouse, especially an unexpected death, is obtaining health insurance for you and your children.

If your spouse was still working, and covered under his or her employer's plan at the time of death, you can continue that coverage for up to three years under the Congressional Omnibus Budget Reconciliation Act (COBRA). Of course, the cost of maintaining the same level of service may be quite high, as you will now be required to pay the employer's portion of the insurance premium, plus an additional 2 to 3 percent administration fee. The main benefit of using COBRA is that you can continue the same service you have been accustomed to while looking at alternatives.

In the event that any new insurance you consider may have a waiting period for pre-existing or other conditions, you can use your COBRA to pay for your health care costs while waiting for the new coverage to begin — at a price, that is. Paying for two separate policies is never cheap, but it is an option in some cases. Maybe you need time to find a job that offers good health insurance, or plan to go back to school temporarily. COBRA coverage can help give you the peace of mind necessary to get through the interim.

For the most up-to-date information on your COBRA rights, contact the U.S. Department of Labor Pension and Welfare Benefits Administrative Division of Technical Assistance and Inquiries, at **www.dol.gov**, telephone: 1.866.4.USA-DOL (1.866.487.2365).

The Types of Insurances Available

If you are considering buying a private health insurance plan, in lieu of taking group coverage from an employer or organization, be sure to investigate all the plans and options available to find the one best-suited to your family's needs and income. When shopping for health insurance, there are several types to look at:

Traditional Health Insurance Plans

Traditional indemnity plans come in two different forms. A basic plan reimburses the policyholder for doctor's visits, prescriptions, outpatient procedures, and other medical expanses covered within the policy restriction and guidelines up to a certain dollar amount each year. Major medical covers all major medical expenses, including emergency room visits, some testing, and both short- and long-term hospitalizations.

Most basic plan holders are required to incur both an annual deductible and/or a service deductible up to a certain amount each year, depending on the individual policy purchased. The most common deductibles range between $500 and $1,500 per person or family, and an 80-20 cost differential, which means that you will be responsible for 20 percent of all service fees. Some plans may offer an annual cap on these deductibles, but not all do, so be sure to read the policy carefully before making a decision.

Like the basic plan described above, most major medical insurance covers 100 percent of any type of inpatient treatment for a specified number of days. After the allotted time, the 80-20 coverage may go into effect. Some major medical policies also offer a per-person or per-family annual cap on deductibles incurred by the policyholder, but not all offer this additional benefit. Another point to consider: Most major medical policies feature a

$1 million lifetime cap on the expenses for which they are responsible. In the event your treatment exceeds that amount, your policy is terminated.

Catastrophic insurance can also be purchased to help cover costs exceeding your major medical policy's lifetime limit. Although pricey, these policies may be a good idea for those suffering with long-term or extensive medical needs. A $1 million dollar policy may sound high, until you consider the high cost of treating someone who has sustained a spinal cord injury, needs an organ transplant, or suffers from certain types of chronic disease. Consider this option carefully if you fall under any of these categories.

HMOs

"Health Maintenance Organizations" have grown in popularity since they were first introduced in the late 1980s. Unlike their previous counterparts, many of today's HMOs offer much more freedom in choosing the doctors you prefer, and some have even eliminated the need for referrals if you see an in-network physician.

One of the main benefits of HMO coverage is the relatively small out-of-pocket expense they require. Most of these plans allow users to see a doctor for a pre-determined co-pay (anywhere from $5 to $60, depending on the plan). This is without regard to the cost of the visit, procedure, or test. The same is true for medications, although some prescription plans may deny coverage for some medications.

Although monthly fees can run the gamut from several hundred to several thousand dollars per month, these plans are much less expensive than a traditional policy's 20 percent deductibles, especially when hospitalization is required. However, if you are a healthy person and do not require many office visits, maintenance medications, or hospitalizations in a given year, the monthly premium of an HMO may appear pricey. Regardless of the cost, health insurance is a must-have in today's world, and an HMO still remains the least expensive option for most.

There are some drawbacks for that more manageable monthly premium price. Some of the disadvantages of an HMO include the following:

- You may not be able to keep your current doctors and/or specialists if they are not an HMO provider

- You may not have access to certain specialists and testing in accordance to certain HMO rules and limitations

- You may need a referral from your doctor, and even permission from the HMO review committee, for certain procedures and treatments

- Some medications may not be available under the HMO prescription plan

- You may be limited to a select few hospitals in which to be treated under the plan

- Some HMOs regularly discourage high-priced testing among its participants, and in some cases, may even deny coverage.

PPOs

Many consumers are now finding the benefits of a Preferred Provider Organization (PPO) hard to pass up. A cross between a traditional medical plan and an HMO, a PPO plan offers the best of both worlds. For a fixed monthly charge — less than a traditional plan and more than an HMO— policyholders can either stay within the PPO network and use its services much like an HMO for a small co-pay, or go outside the network and use the plan in the same manner they would a traditional health care plan, for the same 80-20 payment schedule. While most participants use the plan like an HMO to keep their out-of-pocket expenses low, many admit they like the flexibility of being able to see the doctor they choose and have the tests they want without prior permission of the insurance carrier or a referral by their primary care physician.

Medicare

If you are 65 years of age or older, Medicare is an insurance offered by the federal government to help you maintain your ability to find coverage, despite preexisting conditions and/or your age. There are two types of Medicare insurance:

Part A Medicare – is offered to those who are currently receiving Social Security benefits, regardless of whether they remain in the workforce. The coverage is free for most and covers hospitalization, nursing home care, home hospice, and blood transfusions.

Part B Medicare – covers all your other medical expenses, including outpatient services, testing, prescriptions, medical supplies, office visits, and more. Part B Medicare is not free. Eligible participants must pay a monthly fee for the coverage.

Specialized Health Insurance Policies

In addition to these standard health insurance policies, there is a variety of specialized medical coverage available to consumers. Although they may seem like must-have policies on the surface, many are not needed by the average person. Look at a few of these "extra" insurance policies closer to help you better decide what you need — and what you do not:

Hospital Indemnity Plans. You may have seen their pitch in a television commercial – the policy pays you $75 or $100 a day for every day that you are hospitalized. For those who need the plan to help pay their hospital costs, the plans are worthless, as the average stay costs $700 to $1,000 per day. This varies depending on services provided. The highest cost is $5,000 a day. In addition, these plans rarely pay for pre-existing conditions or for stays shorter than five to ten days. Because most hospitals tend to try to release patients as quickly as possible, many people find that they never qualify for benefits under these plans, and when they do, the reward is minimal at best.

Long-Term Care Policies. If you expected a long-term care policy to cover all the costs of extended nursing home care, you would be mistaken. These policies can be rather expensive and seldom come close to paying all the bills of long-term care. However, if you are looking for a supplement to the coverage you already have, it may be a worthwhile investment, especially if you foresee the need for nursing home care within the next five to ten years.

Supplemental Insurance Policies. Also known as Medigap policies, this type of insurance is designed to fill the gap between what your Medicare Parts A & B pay and what you are expected to pay. With so many different types of Medigap policies now available, through both government and private insurance carriers, choosing the plan right for you (and your budget) can be confusing. The best thing to do is research all the plans and their options carefully before you decide which will best serve your individual needs.

Specific Disease Policies. For those worried about the high cost of contracting a specific disease, they may be tempted to grab hold of one of these policies. Be careful when choosing one, ensuring that it does cover not only the cost associated with the disease, but other ailments that may be caused by the initial diagnosis. Often, these policies are so specific in what they will and will not cover that policyholders are left with little, if any, monetary benefit from the policy or the premiums they paid for the coverage.

> TIP:
> Keep in mind that many states offer a variety of health care programs designed to help single parents and widows fill in their health care gaps. The best way to find out what is available where you live is to make an appointment with your state representative's or senator's office to see how they can help.

Change No. 3: Your Savings and Investments

There are many things to consider about your financial future now that you are once again single, including:

- How to invest your spouse's retirement plan now so that you do not pay too much in taxes or get stuck with too little financial benefit upon your own retirement

- Whether you need to increase your own giving potential now to ensure financial stability when you retire

- What your savings goals are and how they may have changed due to the death of your spouse

- How much risk you feel comfortable taking when it comes to investing

Step No. 1: Figuring Out What to Do with Inherited Retirement Monies

Understanding how today's multifaceted, complicated retirement savings plans are handled can become a nightmare for surviving spouses, especially if they have always let their spouse handle their investments. Many married women, particularly those who left the workforce to raise a family, have little or no idea how much retirement money their spouses had, let alone what types of accounts they were using for their retirement savings.

The first thing you will need to do before you can figure out your next investment move is to figure out what types of accounts your spouse was using to save for the future. The most common include:

The Traditional IRA — An Individual Retirement Plan (IRA) is a type of savings plan that allows you to put away up to $4,000 for your retirement in either a tax-deferred or tax-free account. Although putting money aside in a traditional IRA now can help lower your tax bill now, that money is subject to standard income taxes upon its withdrawal. Another thing to consider is that if you tap into that money before you turn 59 ½, your withdrawal will not only be subject to income taxes, but also a hefty 10 percent penalty.

The Roth IRA — Created in the late 1990s to help middle-class Americans save more for their retirement, this is a non-tax-deductible savings plan (because you pay payroll taxes on the amount applied to the account) that provides more flexibility to its users. First, monies contributed to a Roth IRA can be withdrawn at any time without being subject to any taxes or penalties, though the interest earned on the account can be both taxed and penalized if withdrawn in the first five years. Beginning in 2008, the contribution for a Roth IRA is $5,000.

The SEP Account — Otherwise known as a Simplified Employee Pension Plan, SEP accounts were designed for businesses — both large and small — to offer some sort of retirement savings for themselves and any employees they may have. Contributions to a SEP account are tax deductible and do not require either the business owner or employees to make regular, or even annual, contributions to the plan. This allows small, independent business owners to add money to the account during spikes in business, and stop making contributions during any slowdowns. And with no continuation limits on these accounts, plan holders are free to save as much as they would like. Plus, they are free to withdraw contributions at any time without penalty.

The 401(k) Plan – One of the most popular retirement savings plans offered by employers these days is the 401(k) plan. It not only allows employees to save money for their retirement on a pre-tax basis (meaning you do not pay taxes on money contributed, thus lowering your tax liability with every contribution), but many employers also offer some sort of employee contribution match, giving contributors even more bang for their buck. Plus, the money saved often earns a higher interest rate than independent investing.

Another benefit that makes these plans so popular is the ability to choose your own risk level for any monies you add to the plan. For instance, you may be able to invest in stocks, bonds, annuities, guaranteed investment pools, company stock, or a combination of the options offered in order to create a more diversified portfolio.

Should you need access to your savings at any time, you may be able to withdraw some or all of your IRA contributions (with or without penalty) for any of the following reasons:

- Termination of employment
- Disability
- Reaching age 59 ½ (or 55 in some cases)
- Retirement
- Death

Step No. 2: Taking Possession of Inherited Accounts

There are many options to consider when deciding what to do with an inherited IRA or other retirement savings account. You might think that you simply take possession of the money and invest it any way you like. But though that may be one option, it is not likely the best. Before you make any major decisions regarding what to do with your spouse's retirement monies, look at a few of your options:

Decision No. 1: Whether to Accept This Inheritance

As unusual as it may sound, for some people, especially older widows and widowers, it may be more financially responsible to disclaim, or turn down, your IRA inheritance. Those who find that they can live comfortably on their spouse's other assets, including investments, savings, property, and/or life insurance, may want to consider giving any retirement inheritances to younger benefactors, such as their children or grandchildren. This will enable the new benefactor to maximize the potential of tax-deferred growth over a longer period of time and stretch out required disbursements over his or her entire lifetime, instead of a lump sum inheritance he or she may get upon your death. If you do decide to disclaim your right to any inherited IRA savings, you must do so before taking possession of them, and you cannot change your mind at a later date: The decision is permanent.

Decision No. 2: How to Distribute IRA Monies

If you decide that yes, you would like to keep the inherited IRA, your next step will include transferring the IRA assets to an IRA Beneficiary Distribution Account (IBDA). Once done, you will need to carefully review whatever distribution options are available through the IRA program your spouse was involved in. For most surviving spouses, the main distribution methods include:

- **A Lump Sum Payment** – While it may be beneficial to some to receive the entire IRA inheritance at one time, for most people, the tax cost is simply too high. When taking a lump sum IRA distribution, you are required by federal tax laws to claim the entire amount as income and, therefore, are subject to all regular personal income taxes.

- **Spreading Distributions Over Your Entire Lifetime** – This method allows you to take monthly, or even annual, disbursements over the course of your life, giving you a regular income and allowing you to only pay taxes on the money received that year.

- **Deferring Distributions** – As a surviving spouse, you also have the unique option of deferring all distribution payments until after your 70th birthday.

Decision No. 3: What to Do With a Qualified Retirement Plan

Inheriting money from your spouse's 401(k) or 403(b) plan may not be as straightforward as inheriting a traditional or Roth IRA. Most require you to follow the beneficiary requirements as outlined in the plan. Check with either the plan coordinator or your spouse's employer for details. But do not be surprised if you are forced to either take the entire amount in full or roll it over into another similar type of account until you reach full retirement age to avoid paying high early-withdrawal penalties.

Step No. 3: Investing Your New Retirement Windfall Safely and Responsibly

By now, you have figured out what types of retirement accounts your spouse had and how to get the money. The next step in your own retirement planning is figuring out the best way to invest the money your spouse left you for your future.

If you already have a 401(k) plan or IRA of your own, you may want to consider rolling some (or all) of these new funds right into the plan you already have set up. But for those who were relying on your spouse's retirement plan to sustain both of you in your later years, knowing what to do with this money may be beyond your understanding. To make the best decisions regarding your inheritance and how best to save it, here are a few important retirement investment basics:

Coming to Terms With Your Individual Risk Tolerance

Everyone spends and saves money differently. The same is true for investing. Some people are conservative — happy with less benefit as long as they are certain the benefits are indeed forthcoming — while others opt for more of an all-or-nothing approach to retirement investing. Of course, most of us fall somewhere in the middle: anxious to experience more benefits, but not overly anxious to risk "too much" security.

Determining your own risk tolerance is an important step toward investing wisely, and it should not be overlooked. No matter what the gain, you should always feel completely comfortable with your investment strategy. Listen to advisers you can trust, but be careful not to let others make these important investment decisions; after all, it is not their future financial health at risk. In the end, you are the only one who will reap the benefits of a smart decision — or live with the consequences of a poor one.

Your personal risk tolerance is an emotional gauge. Will you panic if all (or most) of your investments are tied up in stocks and the market takes an unexpected plunge, or are you in it for the long haul, able to handle the ups and downs of an erratic market?

When it comes to risk tolerance, much depends on you and your age. Ultraconservative investors often find themselves feeling jittery and uneasy putting too much of their portfolio into an unstable market, while risk takers do not seem to mind the uncertainty of what their retirement account will be worth from day to day — or even hour to hour. Even risk takers should be careful about putting too much into the stock market within five to ten years of retirement, as any hiccup in the markets or economy can put your livelihood in jeopardy.

There are two main steps to determining your personal risk tolerance:

Step No. 1: Determine how comfortable you are at the thought of losing some of your money.

Step No. 2: Determine how much money you can afford to lose. For instance, if you could live off of 70 percent of your retirement savings, then you may want to consider putting 30 percent into higher yield (and higher risk) investments while keeping the bulk of your money in safer places.

Once you know the answers to these simple questions, you will be able to better see which area of risk tolerance you fall into:

Ultraconservative Investors: This type of investor is looking for more of a sure thing. He or she likes guarantees, even if it means making less profit in the long run. Ultraconservative investors tend to rely heavily on guaranteed investments, such as CDs and bonds.

Fairly Conservative Investors: Although the fairly conservative investor is still uncomfortable sinking too much capital into a high-yield investment strategy, he or she does understand the need to branch beyond his or her comfort level in some degree to benefit the most from investments. Larger cap and dividend-paying stocks are a more comfortable purchase for this type of investor than individual stocks.

Moderate Investors: Moderate investors have the most diversified portfolios, featuring a variety of high- and low-risk investments. They tend to be younger investors who have time on their side when it comes to weathering bad economic times and can afford to lose money today with the plan of making it back again during a market upswing.

Fairly Aggressive Investors: This type of investor is not afraid to take a risk and clearly understands the financial benefits of taking advantage of growth stock cycles and value stock cycles.

Ultra Aggressive Investors: With nerves of steel and a bank account to back it up, this type of investor plays to win. He or she takes high risks, investing in whatever promises the most return — despite the apparent risk involved. He or she is not afraid of losing money, understanding that he or she will gain more in the next round of this high-stakes investment game.

Understanding the Importance of Diversification

When you diversify, you take some money and put it into a higher-risk, higher-yield account; some in a moderate risk account; and the rest in a safer, lower-yield account. That way, while one portion of your savings may be growing steadily at any given point — with the rest growing more slowly over time — you are not risking it all on an investment that may sour at some point.

Once you understand your risk tolerance, you will be in a better position to decide how much of your money to invest in each category.

Determining What You Need to Survive

Sometimes, regardless of your comfort level, you may feel pressured to invest in higher-yield stocks due to a need for faster growth. Although taking more risk can increase your gains at a faster rate, be sure you can afford a downturn, should one occur before you gather your profits and run.

Another thing to consider is what percentage of your inheritance to invest in income-generating investments versus growth-generated investments. For survivors under the age of 50, a good ratio to shoot for is 50 percent income-producing investments and 50 percent growth-producing investments.

If you are looking to use some of your inheritance to live off of now, you will need to purchase some income-generating investments, such as utility stocks; Treasury, municipal, and corporate bonds; or mutual funds.

Growth-producing investments are those that offer long-term profit growth and are excellent sources of raising after-retirement income. Stock mutual funds are an excellent source of growth investments.

Knowing how best to invest your spouse's retirement savings is not going to be easy. After all, you will need to make sure that you have enough to live on comfortably once you reach retirement age. Chapter 8 will address specific savings strategies aimed at surviving spouses. But for now, the most important thing you need to consider is how much you will need upon retirement so that you can figure out how much risk is acceptable now.

By most calculations, experts agree that most retirees will need to have saved between $548,000 for soon-to-be retirees and as much as $3.1 million for the average 24-year-old to continue the lifestyle they have become accustomed to during their working years. If these figures seem staggering, consider that an increasing number of people are living well into their 80s and 90s, making it necessary for their retirement income to last longer than ever before. Add to that projected inflation costs, and younger workers must save even more, as their retirements are decades away.

If you are worried that you will not have enough saved to retire comfortably, some practical ways in which you can boost your savings will be revealed in upcoming chapters.

CHAPTER 3

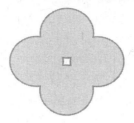

How to Safeguard Your Financial Future Before You File for Divorce

The cost of divorce is staggering: Americans spend nearly $28 billion on the process every year. For those who fail to plan carefully for their divorce, the cost can be high, with devastating effects that ripple through your life for years to come.

Once a divorce becomes imminent, your first step, according to the experts, is to get your own bank account — ideally, one of which your spouse has no knowledge of. It becomes too easy for an angry, hurt partner to use the money in your joint accounts for revenge. Establishing at least a small amount of money on your own can give you the security of knowing that you will have enough to pay for the basics later, should the need arise. Put away a small nest egg to handle your basic expenses for a month or two, should your spouse decide to behave unfairly at any time during your divorce proceedings.

Next, begin taking stock of your current assets and liabilities, and gather the information and paperwork you will likely need. This should include copies of all your most recent financial statements, including bank account statements, investment reports, loans, deeds, property titles, and tax forms.

Be sure to keep these statements in a safe place, away from your current address. The best place for such important documents is a safe deposit box that only you have access to, but you can also leave them in the care of a trusted friend or relative, as long as you are sure that his or her loyalty lies with you.

Using these two important tips to prepare yourself for the financial fallout of your divorce will not safeguard you against an unscrupulous spouse, but it will go a long way toward evening out the playing field in a nasty settlement.

Understanding What Decisions Are Most Important

To protect yourself financially during a divorce, you will need to understand all its aspects, as well as how they will affect your money today and in the future. For many women, the future seems uncertain when divorce becomes a reality. While they struggle to come to terms with their financial survival today, they fail to acknowledge how their divorce will affect their later years.

If you left the workforce prematurely to raise a family, only to discover that your lifetime earnings have left you short of qualifying for any retirement benefits through the Social Security Administration or receiving anything close to a livable allotment, you may be able to collect Social Security benefits using your ex-spouse's income rather than your own.

If you and your spouse were married at least ten years and you never remarry, you can request that the Social Security Administration use your ex-spouse's lifetime earnings to determine your monthly allotment, rather than your own. In most cases, you will be eligible for 50 percent of his or her monthly Social Security benefits total once you reach the age of 62. Of course, this will not mean that your ex will receive less in benefits upon reaching retirement age; it just means that the government will pay both of your benefits using his or her income level.

Understanding Your Divorce Decree and Important Steps to Financial Security

When it comes to protecting your financial security before, during, and after the divorce, another important factor to watch out for is what your divorce decree states regarding shared debt.

During the divorce process, the courts tend to divide the couple's shared debt in a legal divorce decree. For instance, the wife may be given the house and the responsibility of maintaining the mortgage, while the husband assumes all credit card debt and car loans.

Do not make the mistake of assuming that the judge's order is officially carried over in your bank accounts and credit information. Because financial institutions are not party to any legal agreement between you and your ex-spouse, they are not aware of whose fiscal responsibility it is for the debt you currently owe. The best way to avoid any problems in the future is to close out any joint accounts, transfer them into your own name (and make sure that your name is taken off accounts that you no longer are responsible for), and immediately refinance what loans you can. Most divorcées do not realize that they can be held liable for any late payments and/or penalties with a financial institution that has not been informed of the divorce decree.

Getting Professional Help

During the course of your divorce, you may find it necessary to hire one or more different types of professionals to get you through its various stages. The first, of course, will likely be your lawyer. When dealing with divorce, it is advantageous to seek professional counsel, no matter how amicable the split may seem at first; there is no other way to ensure both parties are treated fairly.

Finding a good divorce lawyer can be tricky; it is best to meet with several to see who best meets your expectations. Be wary of those who make big promises or seem to be either too aggressive or too indecisive. You need someone who will do what is necessary to ensure a favorable outcome, without being overly submissive or greedy.

How a lawyer is paid — by the hour, on a retainer, or even on commission — can affect the outcome of your divorce. Remember, it is not to a lawyer's advantage to speed the process, nor to make it too easy.

When paying your lawyer an hourly rate, make sure you clearly understand his or her billing practices. Most bill clients in 10-, 15-, 30-, and 45-minute increments, although some bill partial hours as a whole. That means that if you pick up the phone and ask your lawyer "a quick question," you could be billed for the actual 10 minutes he or she spent speaking with you on the phone — or for a complete hour. It is best for you to limit your calls and questions until you have several to better manage your lawyer's time and your expenses simultaneously. Some other important factors to find out before hiring your lawyer are:

- Whether he or she charges for every phone call
- Whether the clock starts running as soon as you walk into the office
- What incidental time he or she charges for
- Other expenses (such as copies, mailings, filings, and court costs)

Your lawyer should be able to provide you with a clear understanding of how you will be billed and what costs to expect, including retainer fees, court costs, witness fees, and more. He or she should also provide you with copies of all documents related to your case.

Finding a Divorce Lawyer

The first step to ensuring that your divorce does not wreak havoc on your financial life for years to come is finding the right divorce attorney. First, find a lawyer who specializes in divorce. A lawyer who specializes in divorce has a greater understanding of its pitfalls and knows what to watch out for to protect his or her clients. Be careful, though. There are no "rules" or regulations governing when a lawyer may — or may not — call himself or herself a specialist, so find one who can offer references and other proof that he or she has the experience you seek.

Next, look for a divorce attorney with extensive experience *in the state in which you live and in which the divorce will take place.* Ask how long he or she has been in practice and how many divorces he or she handles each year. In addition, make sure that the lawyer you choose has courtroom experience, should you need to go that route. Not all lawyers do. Your outcome may depend on your lawyer's familiarity with the system, the complexities of the process, and what strategies work best with particular judges.

Although court experience is important, also be sure that your new lawyer is well-versed in more amicable options. Flexibility is key when choosing the lawyer to represent you and your needs. You want one with a track record for finding the best solutions and negotiating the fairest agreements for his or her clients.

Just as important as experience is finding a divorce lawyer who knows how to handle individual areas of your particular divorce. If you and your spouse have large investments, find someone who works with financial divorces; likewise, if you fear a custody battle with your ex, then find a lawyer who specializes in custody matters.

Also, be sure your management styles match. Do not recruit a barracuda if you want to mediate a fair agreement.

Finally, find a lawyer you like. If the counsel you choose makes you feel uncomfortable, find someone else. You must be able to trust in this person and his or her ability to get you through this tough situation. If you do not, move on. Otherwise, you risk not getting the settlement you want — and deserve.

Divorce on the Internet

Divorce has changed over the years. With the advent of the Internet — and the many services it offers — it is no wonder some people are turning there for a quick, cheap way to dissolve their marriages. Whether you could benefit from an "Internet divorce" depends on several factors:

1. How long you have been married
2. How much property (if any) there is to disburse
3. Whether there are children (and custody issues) involved
4. How amicable your divorce is

If you do not have any dispute over property or children, then divorce over the Internet can be an easy, fast, and cheaper alternative to high-priced lawyers and their fees. Among the most popular sites that offer completed divorce paperwork are LegalZoom (**www.legalzoom.com**) and CompleteCase (**www.completecase.com**). Charging less than $200, these Web sites can help cut the costs of your split by thousands of dollars. Better than fill-in-the-blank divorce kits, these divorce sites offer individualized guidance and the legal forms required by each of the 50 states, which guarantees that your paperwork will not be denied by the courts. Of course, disputes cannot be handled through these "quickie divorce" sites.

> ## TIP: Divorce Kits Can be a Fast, Easy Way to Free Yourself from an Unhappy Marriage
>
> If you want to avoid the cost and hassle of hiring a lawyer, a do-it-yourself divorce kit may be the answer. Available for as little as $25 to $70, these kits include all the legal forms necessary to navigate the separation of property and other assets, assuming that you both agree on who gets what. Once you fill in the forms, the only step left is to file them with the court and appear before a judge to make your divorce legal and your agreement binding.

Mediation

When you are finding it difficult to agree, sometimes lawyers can get in the way. After all, you have each hired your own counsel to look after your own interests. When it looks like you have reached a stalemate, it may be time to bring in a mediator to ensure that no one loses out in the final divorce deal.

Trained in conflict resolution in family law, a private mediator is a neutral third person who works with both parties to help them reach an agreement on some, or all, of the issues involved in their divorce proceedings. This may include:

- Property division
- Child custody
- Child support
- Spousal support

Mediators are good at hammering out fair, equitable divorce settlements, especially in regard to child custody arrangements. They are experts at determining reasonable compromises and finding solutions that benefit all parties involved.

The major benefit to using a mediator is that it allows you and your spouse to remain in control of making decisions regarding your property and children. In the event you cannot reach a compromise, a judge will make these important decisions for you.

Allowing lawyers to duke out a settlement can be costly, both emotionally and financially. A mediator can either work with your lawyers to explore a variety of options to consider, or he or she can work out the details of your settlement and simply have the lawyers draw up the necessary legal papers. How much involvement you want your lawyer to have is really up to each partner.

Arbitration — Another Alternative

If mediation has failed, and you want to avoid the cost and emotional turmoil of going to court to settle your disputes, consider arbitration. It is more formal than mediation, and less demanding than a court trial.

The important thing to realize here is that if you choose arbitration, you and your spouse will not have the final say over your divorce settlement – the arbiter will. However, set up much like a trial, it will allow you to bring in witnesses, have your attorney speak on your behalf; and provide necessary evidence.

To decide if arbitration is right for you, consider whether you and your spouse:

- Do not want to try mediation (or have and it failed)
- Do not want to run up costly legal bills
- Want to be divorced sooner
- Are willing to let the arbiter make the final decisions regarding your divorce settlement

TIP:

Unlike a judge's decision, which can be appealed, an arbitrator's decision cannot. Once the decision is made, it is legally binding by both parties.

Collaboration Can Offer Less Stress and a Fairer Settlement

When both partners are committed to finding a peaceful resolution and fair divorce settlement, collaboration may be the answer. In this process, spouses are represented by their own attorney; however, they begin the process by each spouse and attorney signing an agreement that states:

- Each spouse agrees to fully disclose and exchange all financial documents that will allow for fully informed financial choices by both parties.

- Both spouses and their attorneys agree to maintain absolute privacy during the process, creating a safe environment for both spouses to freely express their needs and concerns.

- Both spouses agree to reach a written agreement on all issues and forgo their right to have a judge intervene.

- Each attorney may use the written agreement to obtain a final court decree.

- All parties agree that if one spouse ends the collaborative agreement process before they have reached an agreement, their attorney must withdraw from the case and cannot represent their respective clients in a court fight, requiring both spouses to hire new lawyers.

It is crucial to this collaborative process that all parties are committed to resolving their issues without judicial intervention. This no-court agreement is incredibly important, as it provides a major incentive to settle without incurring the cost of starting over again with a new attorney.

Not only is a collaborative divorce easier and more fair for both spouses, but you will also receive important support, expertise, problem solving, and negotiating skills from your attorney, while maintaining control over the negotiation process. It can be a good way to remain focused on finding a positive solution instead of becoming derailed by threats of having to appear in court. It also helps you and your spouse maintain a positive atmosphere and create a cooperative relationship for future co-parenting, which is something many couples lose sight of when in the throes of an emotional divorce.

Finding Other Divorce Help

Your lawyer is not the only divorce help you may want to consider seeking. Considering the high financial cost that ending your marriage may bring, financial planners are playing a bigger role in divorces than ever before. Many divorce attorneys even keep financial planners on-staff to help their clients better prepare for their divorces and provide advice and recommendations on dividing assets and investments.

In addition to ensuring that the couple's assets are divided equitably, a financial planner can also help you better prepare for your financial future as a single person. One of his or her main jobs during a divorce is to help the client identify potential risks in settlement agreements and understand the tax consequences some of his or her choices may cause. Financial planners can also be a good asset when determining a couple's joint worth and cash flow by reviewing their retirement benefits, investment portfolio, and business holdings.

Once your divorce is finalized, a financial planner can be a good asset in helping you set realistic long-term and short-term money goals while helping you develop an action plan to reach important savings and investment milestones.

Some of the things a good financial planner can help you do before, during, and after your divorce include:

- Identify cash flow needs
- Set and stay on a budget
- Evaluate your current investments
- Help you determine which assets you should keep, and which ones you should liquidate
- Offer advice on how to build a solid source of retirement savings
- Evaluate your current insurance needs
- Help you figure out how to best save for your children's college expenses

- Help you make appropriate real estate investment decisions

Pre-Divorce Financial Planning

The following information is excerpted from an article titled "Pre-Divorce Financial Planning: Could This Be the Next Frontier?" written by Carl M. Palatnik, CFP®, CDFA™, CERTIFIED FINANCIAL PLANNER™ practitioner, Certified Divorce Financial Analyst™, and founding president of the Association of Divorce Financial Planners. You can read the complete article at the following Web address: **www.divorceandfinance.org/pre-divorce-financial-planning.php**.

POTENTIAL BENEFITS OF PRE-DIVORCE FINANCIAL PLANNING TO CLIENTS

- More thorough treatment of financial issues
- Better settlements
- Avoidance of mistakes
- Increased likelihood that an eventual settlement will work
- Better understanding of post-divorce financial situations and what might be needed to make them work (reality checks)
- Reduction in emotional distractions and fears and greater focus on financial issues
- Greater focus on needs and paying abilities and less on entitlements
- Greater confidence in results and reduced stress in achieving results
- Empowerment through knowledge, making work sessions more productive
- Acquisition of money management tools, such as proper budgeting
- Increased client optimism for the future

BENEFITS TO DIVORCE PROFESSIONALS

- Same as the client benefits listed above and:

- Reduced liability or concerns about liability
- Reduced stress
- Increased efficiency and productivity
- Reduced need to revisit financial issues
- Increased long-term client satisfaction, potentially leading to additional client work and expanded referrals
- Increased ability to focus on the negotiation process and not get bogged down with the financial issues

ROLE OF THE FINANCIAL PLANNER IN THE PRE-DIVORCE PROCESS

Although most financial planners have the relevant tax and financial knowledge to act as traditional "outside experts," their best contributions come from a more intimate involvement in the divorce process. The broad educational background of the financial planner is ideally suited to this type of work. Because planners have traditionally helped individuals achieve long-term financial goals, *e.g.*, saving for college or retirement, they have specialized training and skills that enable them to analyze financial issues in their long-term economic contexts. During the divorce process, this often sets a more positive and productive tone for discussion; provides reality checks; and empowers individuals to make wise and workable decisions and hard, but often necessary, lifestyle adjustments. It also enables them to address insecurities about financial consequences, power imbalances, and emotional agendas that often impede the decision-making process. The parties frequently feel more comfortable and secure with the choices they are considering, find workable solutions more quickly (often at less cost) and become more aware of post-divorce changes in standard of living, ultimately making them less likely to need to revisit support issues in the future.

WHEN SHOULD THE FINANCIAL PLANNER ENTER THE DIVORCE PROCESS?

The earlier the financial planner becomes involved in the process, the more likely the situation will not escalate out of control, and the more likely good financial decisions will be made. The financial planner can help stabilize the situation, including helping determine short-term support needs or paying abilities, closing or re-registering accounts, changing beneficiaries on insurance policies, notifying credit card companies, or establishing credit.

The [Financial] Planner Can:

- Help the parties translate their goals into workable solutions;
- Determine which proposals are workable or what actions might need to be taken to make them workable;
- Educate the parties about the long-term consequences of specific proposals. This helps the parties feel more secure about the process and more comfortable about reaching an agreement. For example, they should fully understand whether they will have sufficient assets or income to manage their finances, whether they will be able to afford support payments, or whether they will be able financially to survive or prosper over time;
- Suggest alternative scenarios to the parties when necessary.

Used with permission. Excerpted from "Pre-Divorce Financial Planning: Could This Be the Next Frontier?" published in the December 2004 issue of New York Family Law Monthly. Copyright 2004. ALM Properties, Inc. All rights reserved. Further duplication without permission is prohibited.

The Role of Your Insurance Agent

In addition to your lawyer and financial planner, a good insurance agent is a must for newly divorced individuals. New divorcées often continue to carry the same types and amounts of coverage on everything from their home, car, and health to their life insurance policies, even though their life and needs may have changed dramatically. A good insurance agent will sit down with you and go over all your coverage, helping you determine exactly which policies you need — and which ones you do not.

You may be surprised at how much your insurance needs change after a divorce. For instance, while you may have held minimal life insurance coverage before your divorce, you may need to increase it dramatically now that you are your children's primary provider. The same is true for disability insurance. Should you become ill or injured, could you continue to pay your bills on your alimony or child support alone? If not, consider taking out both a short- and long-term disability policy.

Property and car insurances — or at least your deductibles — may also change after a divorce. Review each policy independently and make sure they are all up-to-date and offer the coverage you now need at a price that you can still afford.

> ## WARNING:
>
> Commission-based professionals may try to talk you into policies and services that you neither need nor can afford. While you should always consider their recommendations, be sure to research your need for insurances or other services that you may not have considered before to be sure they are necessary.

The Top Nine Financial Mistakes People Make During a Divorce

The average divorce costs nearly $20,000, and that does not include the thousands that many individuals lose due to poor financial decisions during their divorce. For most, the quicker they can make decisions and have the entire process over with, the faster they can move on with their lives. Unfortunately, not taking the time to consider all the financial impacts those quick divorce decisions will have on your financial life years from now may cause you even more pain in the future. Taking your time to make the right decisions now regarding your divorce and the impact it will have on your finances down the road is an important step. Here are nine of the biggest mistakes to watch out for when hammering out your divorce settlement:

Mistake No. 1: Not Knowing What Your True Living Expenses Are

Few people really know what their monthly expenses are, especially if they have left the family's financial decisions up to their spouse in the past. Be careful not to underestimate your expenses, or you may find yourself agreeing to child support or alimony amounts that you cannot live on. Although budgeting will be addressed in a later chapter, begin the process now by reviewing your spending history for the past two years, and going through what your expected expenses will be now that you are on your own. Do not forget to include incidental costs, like clothing, transportation, entertainment, annual insurances, holidays and birthdays, children's field trips, and school costs.

Mistake No. 2: Assuming That the Custodial Parent Automatically Gets the House

Deciding who gets the house is one of the most emotional decisions a couple can make during a divorce. It makes sense for the custodial parent to try to keep the family homestead to give the children the security they may need at this disruptive time in their lives, but agreeing to keep a house that you cannot afford will only add to your stress and financial trouble in the future. Carefully consider the expense of keeping your home before agreeing to take ownership during a divorce. Otherwise, you may find yourself disrupting everyone's life again in a few years when it must be sold — or, worse, lost to foreclosure.

Mistake No. 3: Believing That Splitting Everything 50/50 is Always Fair

While splitting everything 50/50 may seem like the fairest way to ensure that both partners get their fair share, you must also consider the tax impact of assuming certain assets, the ability to generate income off some assets, and the long-term impact on your financial future by giving up certain property or business assets. Another thing to consider is what time and money each partner put into each asset. Let us take a look at a non-working wife. Her husband may feel justified in keeping all of his business assets to himself because he was the one running the day-to-day operations. But is that fair? Maybe — or maybe not. If you find yourself in this situation, ask yourself: Did I help further his career and/or build his business in other ways, such as taking full responsibility for the home front; working while he was in college or trade school; working during the lean years of his career and/or business start-up; using my own money to help pay start-up costs; and more? If so, you may be eligible for some of his business earnings — either in a one-time payment or in annual profit payments. Every situation and every couple are different. That is why it is so important to consider all aspects before agreeing to any settlement too quickly.

Mistake No. 4: Misunderstanding Alimony and Child Support

One of the biggest mistakes some divorcees make is reducing or ending alimony payments within six months, either before or after a child's eighteenth birthday. If this happens, every alimony payment paid since you were first divorced must be reported as child support, which may not be deducted from your taxable income on your tax return. This can have a big effect on the amount of taxes you owe the government for all reporting years since your divorce.

Mistake No. 5: Misunderstanding Your Debt

Unsecured, or credit card debt, accumulated during a marriage is considered joint debt, unless the credit cards are in one spouse's name only. One thing most divorcées do not realize is that credit card companies will continue to hold you responsible for this unsecured debt, even if your divorce decree names your spouse as the one responsible for paying it off. The best way to ensure that your credit rating does not suffer in the event that your spouse does not pay the debt on time and in full is to contact the credit card company immediately and have your name taken off the account as soon as your divorce is final — or beforehand, if possible.

Mistake No. 6: Misunderstanding Your Spouse's Pension Plan

Find out the current value of all pension plans and other retirement accounts to best determine their worth in both today's figures and in future amounts so that you do not find yourself short-sighted down the line.

Mistake No. 7: Failing to Plan for the Future

Money is the leading cause of divorce, so it is no wonder that money matters carry so much emotion and cause so much distress during the divorce itself. Do not wait to develop a plan for your future. Figuring out how to address savings, retirement, educational needs, insurance, and more *before* your divorce will better equip you to handle what lies ahead. Figuring out how to handle your finances as a single person is not always easy, so be sure to get the professional help you need to ensure success.

Mistake No. 8: Not Looking at the Big Picture

Often, people going through a divorce do not take the time to look at the intricacies involved in their finances and how one decision may affect another. For instance, maybe you have decided to sell your home and split the profits evenly. Have you considered the capital gains hit you will both take? In some cases, it may be better to sell off your share of the house to your spouse so you both can keep as much equity as possible. Be sure to look at the big picture when determining the steps to dissolving your marriage finances to ensure that neither of you lose out.

Mistake No. 9: Failing to Understand How a Divorce Affects Finances

Planning for your future now, while you are still negotiating your divorce settlement, is key to ensuring you will have the money you need to survive your divorce now and thrive later. Do not assume that your life and lifestyle will not change. Anticipate changes and make plans to overcome any obstacles you foresee. Once you sign your divorce papers, the settlement is done and there is no turning back or asking for more — no matter what happens in your life.

> ## DID YOU KNOW?
> ### Fast Facts About Divorce:
>
> Contemplating divorce? Consider these facts:
>
> - Half of all marriages fail
> - If you live with your spouse before marriage (or have a baby), you are more likely to end up in divorce court
> - Financial trouble does not necessarily mean you will get divorced — it actually may increase your marriage's chance of survival
> - Children of divorced parents often have problems such as anger, depression, and low self-esteem
> - Nearly 40 percent of couples who divorce do so within the first 4 years of marriage

Helping Your Children Cope with Your Divorce

Your divorce is not just hard on you — it is hard on your children, too. Here are ten basic ways that you can help your children better deal with the changes your family is undergoing and survive your divorce:

1. **Show Your Children That You Love Them**
    Some children have a hard time separating your disfavor with your spouse and your disfavor with them. Take every opportunity you can to show your children that you love them — despite the pending divorce.

2. **Reinforce to Your Children That it is Not Their Fault**

   All too often, children take the bad things going on in the family and make them their fault. After all, they are the easiest one to blame. If only they had behaved better, or tried harder... Make sure that your children understand that any problems between you and your ex were caused by the two of you and not them.

3. **Encourage Love and Support**

   You might be ready to strangle your ex-spouse, but be sure you encourage your children to stay in contact. Above all else, show them the respect they deserve. Children will mimic your actions, so if you fail to show your ex-spouse respect and concern, they may follow your lead.

4. **Do Not Make Your Problems Theirs**

   Accept that your spouse will have a lasting relationship with the children, and do not talk about your ex in a derogatory manner or complain about him or her in front of your children. Your children have enough to deal with; they certainly do not need to hear you badmouth their other parent — no matter how well-deserved your anger may be.

5. **Get Along**

   Stop fighting in front of your children and try to reach an amicable agreement when discussing child rearing, visitation, and support matters. Otherwise, your children will accept all the blame for your divorce — something that simply is not theirs to take on.

6. **Make Your Children Feel At Home**

   Whether or not your children live with you, be sure to give them a space to call their own and make your new apartment or living space family-friendly.

7. **Respect Their Feelings**

Respect the fact that your children have feelings and opinions about your divorce. Respect what they have to say and what they feel. Whether you agree, they deserve to be heard.

8. **Institute Stability Into Their Lives**

Children thrive on routine. Despite the topsy-turvy changes in their lives, set some priorities and routines regarding homework, bedtime, and family time to help them adjust to their new lives more easily. Smaller children especially find comfort and safety in predicable patterns.

9. **Avoid Being a Super Parent**

You may want to give your children everything they ask for to make up for the mess you and your spouse have made — do not do this. Lavishing children with gifts, trips, and attention will not make them feel better and will only set you up for more trouble in the future.

10. **Delay Dating**

Your children need time to grieve the loss of the family they once knew. Do not introduce a new person into their lives until they are ready — even if it takes longer than you would like.

Divorce Terms to Know

Abandonment – When one person leaves the marriage and home.

Adultery – Sexual intercourse with someone other than your spouse.

Affidavit – A sworn statement made under oath or notarized.

Alimony – Money paid to one spouse from another after a divorce is final.

Alimony Pendente – Spousal support paid during a separation.

Change of Venue – Change of judge or court location.

COLA – Cost of Living Adjustment.

Contested – Any issue that the two parties cannot agree on.

Custodial Parent – The parent who lives with the child.

Deferred Compensation Package – Any monies earned during the years of the marriage. This includes savings, investments, and pensions, as well as salaries.

Discovery – Pretrial disclosure of financial figures, by one or both parties.

Grounds – The basis for which a divorce is sought.

Hearing – A court session held to resolve a legal dispute.

Joint Legal Custody – Allows both parents to continue making joint decisions for their child's education, medical care, religious training, camp, and other day-to-day matters.

Joint Physical Custody – Shared custody in which the child resides in both homes.

Mediation – A non-adversarial process of compromise using a third-party to negotiate.

Motion to Modify – A motion that asks the court to change the current custody agreement.

Motions – An appeal to the court.

No-Fault Divorce – A type of divorce that allows each partner to walk away without taking any blame for the dissolution of the marriage.

Non-Custodial Parent – The parent who does not live with the child.

Petition for Dissolution – A legal petition to the courts asking for a divorce.

Petitioner – The one asking for a divorce

QDRO – An order obtained by the court giving one spouse some of another's pension.

Quit Claim – Giving up your rights to the marital house.

Respondent – The person you are seeking a divorce from.

Retainer – Monies paid to a lawyer for ongoing services.

Subpoena – A summons that requires you to testify in court.

Summons – A written court order requiring your presence in front of a judge.

Visitation – The legal right to see your children.

PART II

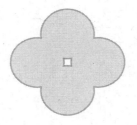

Getting Your
Financial Life
in Order

CHAPTER 4

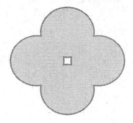

What Do You Owe?
Assessing Your Bills

Whether your financial situation has changed due to the death of your spouse or a divorce, what matters most right now is getting a good handle on what you owe so you can see how that number fits into your current income. Only then can you see where you stand in regard to your money — and what to do about it if you come up short.

Assessing your bills may sound easy; it may seem like all you must do is list all your expenses and add them up. But there is much more to it than that. Few know how much really is spent every month, and now that you must take a good, honest look at your expenses, you may be surprised at how much money leaves your account every month.

Determining What You Spend

Spending money is a fact of life. Problems occur, however, when you have no idea how much you spend. You know the important bills you have, like the rent or mortgage, car payments, insurance, food, and utilities. However, you may not have figured out how much you spend on all those little things that tend to add up to large amounts on a monthly, or even annual, basis. These are expenses such as getting your hair done, giving the children their allowance or field trip money, or those Friday night movie rentals and pizza.

Even if you have a budget, odds are, it does not include everything you spend. If you have enough money in your account to make up the difference, that may be fine, but now that your income has changed, those incidentals may catch up with you if you do not get excess spending under control.

Before the ink is even dry on your divorce papers, or before you have handled the death of your spouse, make it a priority to determine exactly what you spend on a weekly, monthly, or yearly basis.

Most budgeting experts agree that the best way to do this is to keep a daily log of everything you spend for at least a month. This will help you see firsthand where every penny is being spent. An old-fashioned notebook works best. No amount is too small for this list — not even that pack of gum you bought at the gas station.

Once you have your out-of-pocket expense list made, begin listing those expenses that you pay by check or direct withdrawal. Be sure to include bills that are paid once a month, once a quarter, and even once a year. Some areas to be especially mindful of are those forgotten expenses, like professional or personal licenses and registrations, magazine subscriptions, and car inspections. These may seem like small-ticket items, but left to pile up, they can bust a budget in the weeks and months to come.

It is amazing how few people know what they spend on most of the things in their lives. It is easy to hand your teenager $5 for a snack after football practice without realizing how that $5 adds up over time. Even must-have expenses, like parking fees and babysitting expenses, can quickly outpace your income without you ever realizing it — especially when your two-spouse income is suddenly turned into a one-spouse income.

Listing Your Expenses One at a Time

When listing your expenses, start with the big ones first, then go down the line until you are sure that you have included everything. Do not be surprised if your list is extensive, and be sure it includes items such as:

- Groceries
- Rent/mortgage
- Utilities
- Car payments
- School tuition
- Student loans
- Other loans
- Spending money
- Kids' allowances
- School/sports fees
- Club and organization fees
- Gas for the car
- Transportation fees (e.g., licenses, registrations, and maintenance)
- Home maintenance
- Warranty fees
- Health insurance
- Medication costs
- Co-pay and deductibles
- Insurances (e.g., life, home, auto, and disability)
- Home upkeep (e.g., cleaning, gutters, furnace upkeep, mowing, and snow removal)
- Taxes (home and personal)
- Phone
- Cell phone
- Water, sewage, and garbage fees
- Vacation
- Holidays
- Gifts
- Entertainment

- Eating out
- Clothes
- Credit cards
- Lunches
- Child care
- Parking fees
- Rental fees
- Dry cleaning
- Magazines
- Movie/game rental
- Special coffee
- Books
- Alcohol
- Cigarettes
- Grooming products and services
- Postage
- Electronics
- Music
- Computer software and games

Although this may not be an all-inclusive list because everyone's expenses are different, it should give you a good place to start when creating your own.

Categorizing Your Expenses

Once you have your main list complete, it is important to categorize your expenses as either a fixed or variable expense to be able to trim excess spending if necessary.

Fixed expenses include mandatory expenses, such as:

- Taxes
- Savings
- Mortgage/rent
- Utilities (e.g., electric, gas, water, and phone)

- Insurances
- Auto payments, maintenance and repairs, gas, insurance, licenses, and registration fees
- Food
- Clothes
- Medical expenses
- Child care

Variable expenses are those nonessentials or niceties of life that you like to have, but do not necessarily need. They include expenses like:

- Vacation
- Health/beauty
- Entertainment
- Education
- Gifts

DID YOU KNOW?

Most Americans spend between 20 to 40 percent more a month than they need to survive. Do not let that first hard look at your budget intimidate you. The odds are good that there are expenses that you can cut with minimal impact to your current lifestyle. The first step is facing your expenses head-on.

Tips for Calculating What You Should Be Spending

One look at your expenses and you may realize that you are spending far more than you should, or you may simply be wondering whether some areas of your spending are reasonable. What one person may consider excess may be completely normal for another, and that is all right — as long as you can continue to afford it.

Recognizing that it is difficult to know what you should be spending in certain areas, we have compiled some statistics on national averages for you to look over and use to compare with your own spending.

Housing Costs should be no greater than 38 percent of your net income. This includes all costs associated with your home, such as mortgage, taxes, insurance, and utilities, including the phone bill.

Automobile/Transportation costs should not exceed 15 percent of your net income. These costs include loan payments, maintenance, gasoline, insurance, and registration/ inspections.

Food costs should remain under 12 percent of your net income.

Insurance is usually about 5 percent of your net income and includes:

  a. Disability insurance. This helps to cover your daily expenses should you be unable to work temporarily.

  b. Life insurance.

  c. Health. These rates should run between 5 and 15 percent of your net income, depending on the type of coverage and plan you have.

Entertainment and Recreation. Expenses in this category include eating out, sporting events, movies, health clubs, vacations, and theater tickets, and should not exceed 5 percent of your total net income.

Medical and Dental Expenses. This includes medication, co-pays, and annual deductibles, and can be budgeted at about 5 percent of your net income.

Miscellaneous Spending. This is your slush fund to pay for all those incidental expenses (e.g., your morning coffee and newspaper, getting your nails done, and racquetball court rentals) and should remain under 5 percent of your total net income.

Savings. It is best to try to save at least 5 percent of your net income to handle those unexpected emergencies, such as an appliance that needs replacing, a car in need of repair, or an unexpected plane ticket to visit a sick relative.

Indebtedness. It is advisable to keep your debt under 7 percent of your income. This includes any loans you may have, as well as credit card balances.

Budgeting Terms to Know

Allocated Costs – Direct services.

Budget – A plan for spending your money.

Debt Service – What you owe.

Employee (Fringe) Benefits – The costs an employer incurs for your health insurance, disability insurance, unemployment insurance, Social Security benefits, vacation, and holiday pay.

Revenues – Money available including savings and income.

Tax Rate – The amount of tax levied for each $100 of assessed valuation.

CHAPTER 5

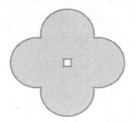

Flying Solo — Learning to Handle Your Finances Alone

If you were lucky enough to have handled your family's finances while still married — or prior to your spouse's debt — then you will not have as much work to do than those who have never picked up a checkbook or paid a bill during their marriage. Either way, there are changes to be made to your finances, and maybe even your lifestyle. But, before addressing how to budget your money, you first need to figure out what type of financial personality you have.

Many things can contribute to your financial personality — and some are positive, some are not. Three of the main characteristics that can lead to indebtedness are:

Ignorance: Being ignorant about your money does not make you unintelligent. It does, however, mean that you lack the financial training that you will need to manage your money well. Acknowledging that you have much to learn when it comes to saving, spending, and investing your funds well is your first step toward gaining the knowledge necessary to live a financially stable, independent life.

Indulgence: If you have an indulgent personality, your desire to have it all can interfere with your ability to remain financially secure. If your spouse was the one who always kept your spending in check, you will need to learn tips and techniques to do it yourself now that you are single again, or you may risk serious consequences in the future.

Poor Planning: This may have left you in some degree of financial hardship after the death of your spouse or divorce. Not taking the time to plan for unexpected emergencies and problems leaves thousands of people struggling financially every year.

Once you know what type of financial personality you have, it will be easier for you to recognize problems before they arise, and take note of situations or decisions that could cause you trouble in the future.

Learning to fly solo in the financial world can be scary at first, but rest assured that you can handle making these important decisions on your own. But before addressing how to invest your inheritance or secure your financial future following a divorce, you must first recognize the importance of reining in your spending and learning how to establish and live on a budget.

What is a Budget, and Why Do You Need One?

Simply put, a budget is an organized plan for managing your finances to meet your financial goals – whatever those goals may be.

Budgets are not meant to restrict your spending; they are meant to free your spending by giving you a way to get everything you want — without the stress of worrying about how to pay for it. That is especially important right now, with your life changing faster than you can keep up. Do not add money woes to your list of worries and stresses. Establish a solid spending plan now to avoid the pitfalls of accrued debt later.

A budget is a guide to keep you from wasting money on the things you do not need so that you can afford the things you do. Few people even attempt to live within their means these days. Often, after a divorce or a spouse's death, the spouse left alone may try and maintain the same lifestyle and spending habits as he or she had as a couple, only to discover too late that his or her income cannot sustain those habits any longer. It may seem old-fashioned to set a budget, especially if you have never done so before, but budgets have many benefits:

They Help You Prepare for the Future: Everyone needs a nest egg, but often, those who find themselves single again fail to prepare for the inevitable: a flat tire, a broken appliance, or a medical expense. Living on a budget can help you to save the money needed for an emergency.

They Give You the Freedom to Spend: If you have never handled your family's finances on your own before, you honestly may not know what you can allow yourself to splurge on. A good spending plan will show exactly how much money you have to spend on frivolous items.

They Create a Sense of Accomplishment: Paying off your debt — no matter how big or small — feels good. Budgeting does not just help you take control of your finances; it helps you take control of your life.

Misconceptions About Budgeting

There are many misconceptions about budgeting that need to be addressed before going any further. After all, if you continue to fight the mere idea of living on a budget due to outdated ideas about what a budget is and what living on one means, you will never be able to move forward in your solitary financial life.

To find out what you truly think about budgets, answer "True" or "False" to the following:

- ***Budgets are only for people with lots of money.*** **False.** Budgeting is more important for those with limited resources, as it helps them see exactly what is going on in their financial life from moment to moment and day to day.

- ***I am not struggling financially, so I do not need a budget.*** **False.** Budgeting allows you to plan your spending surpluses and prevent you from hoarding or overspending.

- ***I am already in debt, so I cannot save.*** **False.** Budgeting allows you to reorder your spending, eliminate excess, begin paying back your debt, and start saving.

Getting Your Expenses in Order

Once you know where your money is going, it is time to come up with a spending plan that better fits your new lifestyle and income. While making your initial expenses list, and prioritizing that spending, you may have noticed a few areas where cuts could be made. Living on a single income again may require reprioritizing your spending several times until you can find a way to live happily on your new income. Those first cuts are the easy ones; it will get more difficult after that.

After cutting the fluff from your expenses, if you still find that you are spending more than you have coming in every month, you will need to make some harder decisions. This can be especially difficult when children are involved, and you are trying your best to keep their lives as normal as possible during this time of change and transition. But do not underestimate the stress that living beyond your means can cause both you and them. Children need to feel safe during any difficult circumstance, and worrying about whether they will have to leave their home or school can cause bigger problems than admitting that you can no longer afford private music lessons, sports activities, and vacations.

There are not any right or wrong answers when it comes to trimming your expenses. If you do not mind trading in your higher-end vehicle for a cheaper, used model, start there. Or maybe you would rather skip expensive treats and trips than downsize your home. What you decide to cut and change is up to you. The important thing to remember is that change is inevitable, especially now that you are single again.

Creating a New Spending Plan

Begin establishing your new spending plan by first prioritizing your expenses, listing the most important ones first. Do not forget to include all the monthly and annual fees that you listed earlier.

Next, divide any non-monthly bills into 12 equal installments, no matter how small they may become. This will allow you to put aside money for taxes, car insurances, and more so that when the bill finally is due, you will have the amount necessary ready and waiting in your account.

According to the U.S. Census Bureau, the average household income in the United States ranges from $43,000 to $48,000 per year. Using this median range, here is a sample budget based on a $50,000-a-year salary for you to study below.

Although the categories and amounts are only suggestions, it will give you a good idea of what types of expenses you will need to include in your own spending plan, and how much is normal:

Payroll Taxes and Insurances	(15 percent)	$708.00
Retirement Savings	(10 percent)	$345.00
Housing Costs *(this includes your rent or mortgage, taxes, insurances, utilities, and maintenance)*	(38 percent)	$1,306.00
Automobile Expenses *(this includes your car loan, insurances, registration and inspection fees, gas, parking, and maintenance)*	(15 percent)	$518.00
Food	(12 percent)	$415.00
Insurance	(5 percent)	$172.00
Entertainment and Recreation	(5 percent)	$172.00
Clothing	(5 percent)	$172.00

Remember: If you have children, you are likely to have other expenses, like diapers, formula, toys, day care, and others that those without kids will not have. That may require adjusting some of the other numbers and ratios within your own personal budget to accommodate these extra expenses.

Five Expenses New Singles May Not Consider

Whether you are now single due to the death of your spouse or a divorce, odds are, you will be experiencing some new and costly expenses. Among some of the most common things you may never have had to pay for before:

- **Private Health Insurance.** If your spouse carried your health insurance through his or her employer, you may find it necessary to take out a private health care insurance after the 36-month COBRA allowance runs out following a divorce or spousal death. While group health care plans may seem expensive, they are nothing compared to the cost of carrying private health care or eye and dental coverage. The average full health care policy runs between $700 and $2,500 per family of four, depending on the type of policy and coverage you choose.

- **Child Care.** If you have always been a stay-at-home mom, you may never have had to pay for before-school, after-school, or day care for your children. This is a new expense that you will likely incur if you must return to the workforce following your divorce or the death of your spouse. Full-time childcare can run between $600 and $1,500 per month, per child, depending on the facility you choose. Even private babysitters can be costly, ranging from $100 to $300 per week for each child.

- **Retirement Savings.** If you have never saved for your own retirement, and your divorce settlement or inheritance was not enough to put some retirement monies away for your future, you will need to open an IRA and/or 401(k) plan immediately to ensure you have enough to live on during your elder years. Average contributions for those older than 30 should be between 3 and 15 percent of your gross salary, or at least $5,000 per calendar year.

- **Disability and Life Insurances.** Now that you are your family's sole caregiver and provider, you need to think about what would happen to you and your children should you be out of work for any length of time or die unexpectedly.

- **Moving Expenses.** In some cases, you may find it necessary to move from your current home as your financial situation changes. Moving incurs some cost, as you will be responsible for paying for rent and security deposits and utility hookup fees in your new home, plus whatever it costs to hire a mover or rent a moving truck and do it yourself.

BUDGETING 101: Five Simple Steps to Setting Up Your First Budget

Budgeting is not difficult, but it does take some work. Although there are no solid rules involved in creating a budget that works for you and your family, you will need to devise a plan that fits your income, even if that means changes to some of your lifestyle habits.

To create a budget you can live with, begin with these five simple steps:

1. **Keep a List of Every Household Expense for One Month**
   Everyone has a clear idea of the big bills: mortgage, car loans, and groceries. The little things are what can throw you off-track. By listing every expense for a set period of time, you can get a better idea of what you are spending.

2. **Compare Your Expenses to Your Income**
   Once you have listed all your expenses, it is time for the hard part: comparing what you spend with the money you have available.

3. **Be Realistic**

   If you are spending more than you make, it is time to get real: You simply cannot continue on this spending path without serious repercussions. Sooner or later, you will not be able to pay your bills and will have to deal with your spending habits; get real now, before you find yourself in a financial hole too deep to climb out of.

4. **Develop a New Spending Plan**

   Begin by prioritizing your spending. Cut out all nonessentials until you can either figure out how to increase your current income or pare down a few bills.

5. **Stick With the Plan**

   No one said it would be easy to stick to a budget, especially if you never had to before. But your life is different now, and that may mean some sacrifice on your part, at least for now. That does not mean that you will have to live like a pauper forever, but it may mean scaling back temporarily until you can figure out a better way to handle your current debt and spending. Changing your spending habits is never easy, but it is possible. You can do it, with the right attitude and the right tools.

The Things That Kill a Budget

Imagine being able to cut your expenses in half. Statistics show that you can. Most middle-class Americans can live on half of their income without giving up any of life's necessities, simply by tweaking their spending habits. Think that is impossible? Consider trying out some of these cost-saving measures:

Stop Wasting Money for Things You Don't Need (or Really Want)

All of those simple frivolities can really add up (especially when there are several people in a household who are indulging in them). Think about all of the money you waste in a week, a month, and a year on small things you would not really miss should you give them up. That does not mean that you cannot enjoy special outings or activities. But you will need to trim the excess to survive financially, which may mean buying a new spring wardrobe every other year instead of every year. Sometimes, making simple changes, like limiting each child to one extracurricular activity, club, or sport per season, can make a big difference in how much money you have to spend on the things you really need.

Look For Cheaper Alternatives

There is almost always a cheaper way to do something. You can buy generic, or find a new store to shop at. Maybe your family would like to try their hand at camping instead of vacationing at a resort. Finding different ways to buy the things you want or to do the activities you enjoy can make a big difference on your wallet — and your bank account. Here are a few places to start saving big:

- Do not buy another DVD when you can rent or, better yet, borrow the ones you want to see for free from a friend.

- Eat a little earlier at your favorite restaurant. Eating during the early-bird offering instead of peak dining hours may only cost you half of what you are used to spending for a meal out.

- Try vacationing during the off-season. It is often much quieter and cheaper.

- Use coupons. It does not matter whether you are buying furniture, appliances or clothes; most stores offer coupon deals from time to time.

Never Pay Full Price Again

Everything goes on sale. Why not take advantage of those sales? If you happen to purchase something at full price, stash those receipts in case it goes on sale later. Most stores these days offer a price guarantee, which allows you to take in your receipts within 30-60 days, and be paid back the difference between what you paid and what the item goes on sale for.

Cutting back your expenses is not always easy, and sometimes it even requires making some big changes. If you are trying to cut your current bills by thousands of dollars every year, try these tips:

- Move to a smaller house. Downsizing can save you hundreds of dollars every month on rent (or a mortgage), maintenance, taxes, and even insurance.

- Buy an older car. Get rid of your new wheels (at its payment) and buy a cheaper model instead. You will not only save on car payments, but insurance costs, too.

- If it costs you money to keep, ditch it. Get rid of anything that costs you excess money to maintain, like such as a pool, RV, or boat.

- Stay home. Try taking a few day trips instead of a big resort vacation. You may be surprised at how relaxing (and fun) stay-at-home vacations can be.

Why Budgets Fail

Unfortunately, many people ditch their budgets before they have ever given them a chance. According to the experts, most budgets fail because of:

- **A Poor Attitude**
  Maybe you are angry that you have been put into a situation that requires you to limit your spending, and you plan on fighting these changes no matter what. If so, you are poised to fail. Be careful that your attitude does not sabotage your efforts to realign your spending with your current income.

- **Motivation**

  Many people fail to ask themselves the "why" behind their need to change their spending ways. If you are being forced to embark on this financial journey, you may lack the motivation to give it a healthy try. Do whatever you can to motivate yourself to make a plan and stick to it to ensure that you remain on financially secure ground for decades to come, despite the tragedy that has befallen you today.

- **Expectations**

  Budgeting is not a quick fix — it is a permanent way of thinking about the way you spend your money. Do not expect miracles when it comes to changing old habits or making your money last for longer than it can. The reality is that budgeting is not a sprint, but an endurance race. Begin with some reasonable expectations and a manageable pace, and you will reach your financial milestones — no matter what your situation.

- **Contentment**

  It is no coincidence that those with enough money to meet their basic needs, but not enough to overindulge in frivolousness, are less stressed, and often more content, than those who can afford big vacations, luxurious homes, and countless activities. They have learned the No. 1 lesson in life: Things do not equal happiness. Do not confuse your own happiness with your ability to buy things.

- **An Inability to Cut the Excess**

  Too often, people mistakenly believe that the extra niceties of life are necessities. Face it: You do not need that gym membership or that private school. They are nice, but you and your children will not perish without them.

- **Never Substituting**
  Do not scoff at buying generic, staying in a low-end hotel on vacation, or driving a used car. Get used to it. If your income has been downsized, expect your lifestyle to do the same.

- **Paying Full Price**
  Eventually, most things go on sale, and refusing to wait until the price of the item you want is slashed 10, 20, or even 50 percent is a big mistake.

- **Failing to Consider Big Changes**
  When debt has overburdened you, it may be necessary to consider some of these big-time changes in the way you live and spend money:

  - Downsizing your home
  - Selling your car(s)
  - Get rid of anything that costs you money to upkeep
  - Ditch the pricey vacation — stay home instead.

As you can see, there are many things that can kill a budget. Be careful when planning how you spend your money to be sure that every expense is a justifiable one that is not going to cost you more in the long run than it is worth.

Top 11 Money-Saving Tips Everyone Should Use

There are many simple ways to save money. Most are personal: Some people may opt to switch to generics, while another would rather take the bus to work once a week. What spending changes you decide to make are up to you, but here are a few to get you started:

Tip No. 1: Use Cash Only.

A simple way to eliminate overspending is to always pay with cash.

Tip No. 2: Never Pay Full Price

Do not buy anything unless it is on sale.

Tip No. 3: Use Coupons/Rebates

Coupons and rebates are everywhere, if you look. From your mailbox, weekly newspaper, or computer to the stores themselves, coupons and rebates can be found for virtually any item, large or small. If you cannot find one, ask the retailer for one.

Tip No. 4: Increase Your Insurance Deductibles

Save 3 to 15 percent on your home and auto premiums by increasing your deductibles to $500 or $1,000.

Tip No. 5: Downsize

From your house to your car, downsizing can have a dramatic effect on your bottom line.

Tip No. 6: Do It Yourself

Never pay someone to do something that you can do yourself.

Tip No. 7: Get Rid of Your Credit Card Balances

You may be amazed at how much you spend every month on credit card interest. Combine all your balances onto one low-interest card, if possible, and make one smaller payment.

Tip No. 8: Eat In

Eating out, including the quick bagel and coffee in the morning and lunch in the afternoon, can add up. Start eating breakfast at home, pack everyone's lunches, and limit your restaurant experiences to special occasions.

Tip No. 9: Get Rid of Unnecessary (and Unused) Services

Take a look at every bill that comes into your home. Does your phone bill contain fees for special services that you neither want nor use? How about the cable bill? Do not forget those banking fees. Stop using the ATM and paying a fee for the privilege; use automatic bill paying to eliminate those late fees because you forgot when the water bill was due; cancel the "extra" channels on your cable or satellite system; and get rid of any phone, TV, or other services that may be costing you money, especially if you rarely use them.

Tip No. 10: Learn to Say "No" Once in a While

The word "no" is not a death sentence, even though your children would like them to believe that it is. Start saying "no," and see your wallet size grow.

Tip No. 11: Go Green

Becoming more energy-efficient in everything you do can save you hundreds of dollars every month on your utility bills. Some simple ways to save big include:

- Shutting off lights when you leave a room
- Making sure the computer is turned off throughout the night
- Unplugging unused appliances
- Keeping your car well-maintained, which saves gas
- Avoiding unnecessary errands or bundling errands together
- Hanging your clothes out to dry on nice days

Re-Establishing Your Credit

Though learning how to budget and spend your money responsibly is important to flying solo in the financial world, re-establishing your own credit is equally important, but it is often overlooked by recent widows and divorcées.

As a married person, you had joint bank accounts, which likely included credit cards, car loans, a mortgage, and more. One of the biggest credit mistakes spouses make during their marriages is assuming that being an authorized user of an account helps them build their own credit. The truth is that if you are not listed as a responsible party on the account, it does nothing to build your own credit rating or establish an independent credit history.

Maybe you have had a few smaller accounts in your own name over the years, like a store credit card, but these may have done little to build an independent credit history apart from your spouse, unless they were used regularly. Now that you are on your own again, it is crucial to re-establish your own personal credit history and scores.

DID YOU KNOW?

The Federal Trade Commission states on its Web site that the federal law regarding credit terms does not allow any creditor to close a joint account without spousal permission following a divorce or separation. It is important to have these accounts closed quickly to avoid any detrimental effects on your personal credit scores due to an ex-spouse's abuse of the accounts.

After a divorce or the death of your spouse, if you are finding it difficult to obtain credit on your own merits, you may need to take some time to try and re-establish a solid credit rating as a single person. Giving your credit score a resurrection is not always easy, but it can be done, with a bit of smart financial work on your part.

Determining Your Credit Score

The first step toward rebuilding your own credit is to check your credit score. This can be done by contacting one or more of the three main credit reporting agencies that track credit scores in the United States:

1. Experian: **www.experian.com**
2. TransUnion: **www.transunion.com**
3. Equifax: **www.equifax.com**

These agencies are required to provide you with one free credit report each calendar year. You are required to pay for additional copies. Fees range from $10 to $25. A credit score is important if you ever plan on getting a credit card or taking out a loan on your own.

Credit scores are used by lenders to determine how much of a risk they are taking by lending you money. Never underestimate how a low credit score will affect your ability to borrow money in the future. The national credit score average is 723, with 850 being the highest level attainable. Scores below 650 are considered poor and can make borrowing difficult.

In addition to making it hard to get the money you need, especially for larger purchases like a house or car, a poor credit score can also affect how much of a down payment you will need for your purchase, what your interest rate will be, how long you can take your loan for, and a variety of other loan terms.

The most common form of credit scoring used by lenders is called a FICO score. FICO is the acronym for Fair Isaac Corporation, the company that devised this credit checking system in the United States. A person's FICO score is a statistical calculation that tells a lender how credit-worthy you are by showing a likelihood of default.

There are three main credit reporting agencies that supply FICO scores to lenders: Equifax, Experian, and TransUnion. Although each is a little different in the way they provide FICO score information, they all mean about the same thing and do not differ by more than 50 points.

These companies determine your individual credit score by evaluating the following:

- 35 percent – payment punctuality
- 30 percent – your total debt and its ratios between your revolving credit (credit cards) and total available credit
- 15 percent – length of credit history
- 10 percent – types of credit used
- 10 percent – recent loans and amounts secured

Although your current income and employment history do not influence your FICO score, they are considered when applying for any loan.

Unfortunately for many new singles, the criteria used to develop their credit scores leaves them with lower-end scores simply because they have not taken the time in the past to keep a certain percentage of their family's debt and credit in their own name throughout their marriages, making it necessary to play catch-up after their spouse dies or leaves.

There are several good ways to begin to re-establish your own credit:

1. **Apply For a Secured Credit Card.** If you are finding it difficult to qualify for a regular credit card, set up a secure account, which requires you to front the money for your card limit up-front. That way, if you default on your payments, the credit company can request payment from the secure line.

2. **Get a Non-Secure Credit Card.** Keep your balances low and make your payments on time for the fastest benefits.

3. **Apply For a Non-Secured Personal Loan.** Borrowing just $1,000 over a 12-month period can help you prove that you can responsibly borrow money and handle the payments. In the event that the bank

requires a co-signer for the loan, ask someone you trust to guarantee the loan, and as soon as it is paid off, reapply for a new non-secured one, as taking all the financial responsibility will do more to build your credit than carrying a secured or co-signed loan.

4. **Apply For Store Credit.** No matter what you are buying, use store credit in the early days of credit building. Just make payments on time and pay off the balance quickly, as interest rates and penalties can be quite high.

No matter what the circumstances, building — or rebuilding — your credit cannot be an instantaneous process; it can often takes years. But with diligence and patience, you can slowly build the credit history and obtain the credit scores that you will need for a solid financial future.

In the event that your divorce or widowhood has left you in more debt than you can handle right now, you may want to consider using a credit counseling agency to help you get your debt under control and strengthen your FICO score.

Credit counselors are good at helping those in serious financial strife eliminate some of their debt by working as their client's advocates to get creditors to forgive interest and penalties that have accrued on accounts and offer a faster way to pay off their balances to rebuild their credit.

Although many credit counseling agencies charge hefty fees for their services, there are hundreds of non-profit groups throughout the nation that provide the same level of service for free or at a reduced rate. Check your local yellow pages for an agency near you.

If you cannot afford, or do not have access to, a credit counseling agency, there are ways to fix your problems yourself. A few basic things you can do on your own to begin repairing your credit include:

• Closing all joint accounts.

- Notifying all your creditors about your situation, and making sure that they begin recording your credit history separately from your spouse's.

- Disputing any disparities in your credit report.

- Being certain that your credit report includes accounts held in your maiden name prior to your marriage.

- Trying to distance yourself as much as possible from your spouse's poor credit practices.

- Asking any creditors who appear amicable to have your name deleted from any negative credit reports with accounts handled by your spouse.

Repairing poor credit is not going to be easy, but it can be done. The key to establishing — or re-establishing — your personal credit is being patient, persistent, and responsible from now on. There is no room for making mistakes for the time being, so be sure to make every payment on time until you have had time to rebuild a credit history and rating on your own.

CHAPTER 6

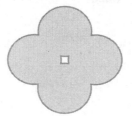

Borrowing Smart
on Your Own

Consumer credit debt is at an all-time high. Now that you are on your own again, it is important for you to understand the risks and benefits of borrowing money, both now and in the future.

Although it is true that borrowing can help you get what you want and need now, it comes at a price — sometimes a high price. The interest you pay on your debt is one way to get in over your head quickly.

The Facts on Interest

Many people have discovered the dangers of interest in the last few years, as interest on their mortgages doubled, tripled, or even quadrupled when their low-interest mortgages suddenly re-adjusted to levels that bumped their payments beyond their ability to cover the new higher costs.

The more money you borrow, whether for a car, a house, or simply day-to-day expenditures, the longer it will take to pay it back, and the more interest you will have to pay. Of course, the type of interest you must pay on your loans (including credit cards, which are loans of sorts) depends largely on the type of money you are borrowing, and for how long. Here is a rundown of the most common types of loan and credit card interest you may be expected to pay:

Fixed Rates

Fixed-rate loans are the best type of loan to take, if possible, because with this loan, your payments can never go up. This can be an important factor, especially on large loans, such as mortgages. When taking out a fixed-rate loan, you (the borrower) agree to pay a certain percentage rate for the life of the loan, for a certain period of time, and your payments are figured out from there. When borrowing money for a car, most loans run between three to seven years, homes run between 15 to 30 years, and personal un-secured loans run between one to ten years.

There are drawbacks to fixed-rate loans under some situations. For one, if interest suddenly drops, you will be stuck with your interest rate unless you refinance the loan. If you decided to pay off your loan early, you may be required to pay a pre-payment penalty. Check your loan agreement for a clause about pre-payment penalties to see whether this penalty applies to your loan.

Adjustable Rates

With so many different types of adjustable rate loans available these days, it may be difficult to know what is different about each. They all share some common characteristics. First, they offer a lower "starter" rate. After a certain period of time, the loan resets itself to a higher rate – and higher payments. Some adjustable rate loans adjust annually, while others reset more often — quarterly or even monthly.

Interest-Only Loans

Interest-only loans are most often offered for big-ticket items, like new cars, homes, or furniture and appliances. As its name implies, the interest-only loan allows the borrower to put off making principal payments on the loan for a pre-determined amount of time (about a year) at the beginning of the loan. While a good way to buy larger items right away and enjoy smaller payments at first, it does lengthen the life of the loan.

Special Home Loans To Consider

When buying a home, there are three special types of loans you might want to consider:

FHA Loans

After a divorce or the death of a spouse, you may not have the money to afford closing costs on a new home. That is where The Federal Housing Authority (FHA) may be helpful. They make home loans available to people who may not otherwise be able to come up with enough down payment at reasonable costs or closing cost monies to purchase them otherwise. Although borrowers are required to have good credit and a provable income to qualify for a FHA loan, the mortgage requirements are less stringent than with other, more traditional loans.

VA Loans

VA Loans are provided by the U.S. Department of Veterans Affairs and, like the FHA loans, they have more lenient requirements for borrowers. They are available for veterans of the U.S. Armed Forces and their surviving spouses.

Combo or 80/20 Loan

This is an option for homeowners with no cash available for a down-payment, which is often the case for new singles. The combo or 80/20 loan is two separate loans. The first is a fixed-rate, 30-year mortgage for 80 percent of the home's price, while the second is an adjustable-rate (ARM), ten- or 15-year loan that is used to pay the balance.

Although it can help a cash-strapped buyer get into a home, there are drawbacks to using this type of financing, and it should be considered carefully.

Remember, the 20 percent loan carries an adjustable interest rate that will likely increase over the life of the loan, which could raise your payments higher than your ability to make them comfortably.

Mortgage Terms You Should Know

Amortization schedule – A schedule for payment that outlines to the borrower how their payments will be allocated in regard to principal and interest.

Balloon Payment – A type of loan that requires one large payment after a period of time to pay the loan off in full.

Reset – What happens when an adjustable mortgage's interest rate changes.

Getting a Loan

Now that you are single again, you may find it necessary to borrow money for big-ticket items, such as a car, furniture, and educational expenses. Taking out a personal loan may be the answer. This type of loan is easier to secure, and does not require any type of collateral – except in the case of a car, where the lender will likely hold the title until the loan is paid in full.

Here is a quick rundown of some of the most popular choices available by today's lenders:

Car Loans

Car loans can be used to purchase a new or used car, and typically run between $5,000 and $55,000, depending on the make and model of the car being purchased. Terms run one to seven years and can feature a fixed or variable rate, although a fixed-rate loan is usually preferred.

Unsecured Personal Loans

An unsecured loan allows good credit risks to borrow money without offering any type of collateral. The lender relies solely on the borrower's good credit history to make the loan available. Unsecured personal loans range from $1,000 all the way up to $100,000 and are most commonly paid back within five years.

Equity Line of Credit

If you own your home, an equity line of credit can give you the flexibility of borrowing money when you need it. An equity line of credit offers a set amount of money available to the borrower to use any time, for any purpose, simply by writing a check off of the account. The major benefit of using this type of loan option is that interest will only accrue on the amount borrowed, not the amount approved. As it is secured by the borrower's home, this type of loan program should be used with caution because failure to make your payments could result in the loss of your home.

Tips to Choosing a Personal Loan

When choosing a personal loan option, consider these important tips:

- *The Interest.* Interest on personal loans can be outrageous, ranging from 11.95 percent to 20 percent or more. How your interest rate is calculated depends on the lender, your current credit rating, how much you need to borrow, and the terms of the loan.
- *The Term.* Most personal loans come in terms of one, three, five, seven, and ten years. Pick the term that best suits your comfort level and budget.
- *Penalties.* Some people take out a loan with the thought of making extra payments to pay it off early. If this is something you are planning to do, be sure that your lender does not charge any type of prepayment penalties or fees. Otherwise, you may negate any savings from making an early payoff.

Credit Cards

After a divorce or death, you may find yourself reaching for your credit cards more often. Credit card debt is on the rise — and not just among the newly single. It is estimated that most American consumers carry between five and ten individual credit cards in their wallets at any given time, and have more than $5,000 in credit card debt. Those are numbers that should scare any credit card consumer.

Although they may be necessary at times, credit cards should not be your standard way of paying for purchases. That said, there are occasions when you must use your credit card. That is why it is important to know how your cards work, and to figure out which one is best to use for certain purposes. The most crucial factor to look at in regard to the credit cards you already have (and those you will likely get in the future) is your *interest rate*. Here are a few things to watch out for:

Interest-Free Days

Many credit card companies offer interest-free account days. These allow consumers to make purchases and pay no interest, as long as their bill is paid in full each month. It is a good way to "buy now – pay later," without the penalty.

Ongoing Interest

Cards featuring an ongoing interest rate charge interest no matter what. Charged from the day you make a purchase until the balance is paid in full (even if you pay your account in full every month), an ongoing rate applies to every purchase you make. Of course, the faster you pay off the balance, the less you will ultimately pay in interest. One benefit of this type of card, especially when making bigger purchases that will take awhile to pay off, is that they carry a lower interest rate than other cards.

Penalties

Penalties are a type of additional interest that is charged to your account if you are late — even by an hour — on your payments. They can be high and should be avoided.

Choosing a Credit Card

No matter how good or bad your credit, odds are, you are a regular receiver of notices that say, "You are approved!" Credit card companies have become good at soliciting new business in recent years, combining offers and teaser rates to draw in customers. With so many options and marketing ploys out there, it is not always easy to figure out which card is best. The most important thing to consider when choosing a credit card is to evaluate the amount of debt you can comfortably manage and apply for a credit limit up to that amount – and that amount only. The credit agency may say that you qualify for a $10,000 card limit, but if you only want $5,000, decline the rest. Besides, you can always ask for more later if your circumstances change.

Here are some other tips to consider when choosing a credit card:

- **The Places You Are Most Likely to Shop.** If you like to shop at specific stores, choose in-store credit cards, but if you like the ability to shop wherever you want, go for a more generic MasterCard or Visa. One note here: Store credit cards often feature a higher interest rate, but may offer other perks, like special discounts or bonus savings.

- **The Interest.** Always look for the lowest (permanent) interest rates. The higher the rate, the more you will pay for your purchases. High interest cards can increase your monthly payments, making it more difficult to pay them off quickly.

- **The Other Fees.** Credit card companies charge many different kinds of fees: annual fees, service fees, cash advance fees, and high late fees, among others. These special add-on fees are designed to create more income for them, and less paying power for you.

When shopping for a new credit card, be sure to always check card companies carefully and read their terms of use agreements thoroughly.

Getting Out of Credit Card Debt

It is not rare to find yourself in credit card trouble without even realizing it, especially at a time in your life where everything is in turmoil – including your finances.

As of April 2009, the average adult debt is $4,013, and average household debt is $7,861. More than half of credit cardholders owe more than $20,000 to their credit card companies.

If you find yourself drowning in credit card debt, take action. Begin to dig your way out of this mess by taking the following steps:

1. **Stop Using Your Credit Cards Right Now.** You cannot get out of debt until you stop accruing it.

2. **Consolidate Your Debt Onto One Low-Interest Card.** But watch out for high cash advance or transfer fees.

3. **Cancel All Unused Cards.** Although it may negatively affect your credit rating temporarily, it will help you to eliminate the ability to accrue more debt in the future.

4. **Use Cash.** It is a proven fact: You spend less when you use cash.

5. **Stop thinking of your credit card as cash.** It is not. They always cost more.

6. **Pay Your New Balances in Full Each Month.** Never buy anything with a credit card that you cannot pay off at the end of the billing cycle.

7. **Pay Off Your Highest Interest Cards First.** Begin by paying off your highest interest card first, no matter what the balance. The interest you save on that card can be put toward the balances of the next one.

8. **Always Pay More Than the Minimum Payment Required.** Minimum payments are designed to keep you in debt by leaving nothing to pay down your principal. Plus, the interest owed may increase your balance every month

9. **Always Pay the Amount of the Interest, Plus More.** This is the best way to attack your principal.

When it is Time to go House Hunting

Whether you lost your home in your divorce settlement or have to downsize after your spouse's death, you may find yourself in the midst of buying a home soon.

It does not matter if it is your first house or not: Buying a home can be complicated and expensive. Making matters worse is that you have to do it all alone this time. Consequently, there are many things to consider before taking this important leap into home ownership.

Pick up any newspaper these days and you will read horror stories about people losing their homes. The key to obtaining a mortgage you qualify for and have the ability to pay is being prepared. To get prepared, learn what the mortgage process is all about.

The First Step

Before even looking at houses, the first thing you should do is figure out whether you are ready for the responsibility of owning your own home alone. Consider yourself a first-time homebuyer. After all, the last time you did this, you had a spouse to handle some of it. Think about the time and money you must put into a home. Are you up for it? Who will handle maintenance and repairs? Can you afford to hire them out, or will you have to go it alone? Can you fix a leaky faucet, mow the lawn, keep the snow shoveled, or even paint a room by yourself? If not, factor the cost of hiring someone to complete those tasks in addition to your monthly mortgage payments.

Here are a few important questions to ask yourself when considering buying your first home on your own:

- **Is My Income Steady?** If your income is sporadic, such as those who are self-employed, seasonal workers, and those who work on commission, you may find handling the costs of a home too much to bear right now.

- **Am I Planning on Staying Put For a Few Years?** If there is even a slight chance that you may be moving out of the area in the next five years, it is not a good idea to invest in a home right now.

- **Do I Have Enough Money to Handle Down Payment and Closing Costs?** Ask your realtor for an estimate of these costs on the type and cost of house you are considering. Most home buyers underestimate the costs of buying a home and fall short when they realize how many surplus fees are added at the closing table.

- **What is My Emergency Fund?** Emergencies happen; have at least three months' salary set aside to handle any big emergencies that may come your way after purchasing a home.

- **Am I Debt-Free?** Be sure that all your debt is under control before taking on such a large loan as a mortgage. You are your sole bread winner now. If something happens to you or your income now, you are in trouble.

The next step is figuring out what you can afford. Mortgage brokers are a good place to find out what you qualify for, though only you know what you can truly afford. Unlike a loan officer, who is forced to find a loan within his or her specific bank or lending agency's loan options, a mortgage broker is free to investigate as many financial institutions and lending options as they like in order to find you the best deal.

When meeting with any lending agency, be prepared to answer many questions, including everything imaginable on your overall financial picture, your debt ratios, and your income. How much money they are willing to give you will depend on several factors:

- Your income
- Your current expenses
- Your estimated home expenses
- Your credit rating

Be prepared to explain why you may have had a lapse in your work history, and what has changed in your life over the last two to five years. They will also order a complete credit report, which will highlight any discrepancies or late payments on all your bills. The best time to check for errors in your credit report is before your first meeting with a loan officer. Once the loan officer finds a problem, he or she will be obligated to report it, but if you find and fix one, he or she never needs to know.

Home Warranties Can Offer Peace of Mind

For a relatively small fee (about $500 to $700 a year), a homeowner can purchase a home warranty that enables him or her to have most major appliances and plumbing and electrical issues fixed by one of the warrantor's contractors for a small deductible. Check with these popular home warranty companies for more information:

- American Home Shield: **www.ahswarranty.com**
- National Home Protection:
  www.nationalhomeprotection.com
- The Warranty Group:
  www.thewarrantygroupdirect.com
- First American Home Buyers Protection Corporation:
  www.homewarranty.firstam.com

Applying for Your Home Loan

Once you have figured out how much mortgage you can afford, and what type of loan best suits you, it is time to fill out a loan application. This can take a while, with most loan processes taking anywhere from two weeks to two months until your mortgage is finally approved. How quickly you can obtain a mortgage depends largely on how fast you can get the necessary documents together. Once you complete the necessary paperwork and hand in all documentation requested, an appraisal must be scheduled for the property you are considering. If you are applying for a pre-approval before house hunting, then the appraisal can wait until you find a property.

Once complete, the entire package will be sent off to the lender's underwriters for review and approval. Depending on the circumstances, and the underwriters' criteria, you may be asked to clarify certain items on your application or found in your credit report/history.

As soon as your loan is approved, you are free to set a settlement date for closing on your new home, although some real estate agents set the closing date prior to the actual approval.

If you have a steady income, low debt ratios, and at least 10 percent cash that can be used for a down payment, the odds are that you will find the entire mortgage process fairly easy and void of stress. Unfortunately, that is not the case for most. Those without perfect credit histories and little money can find the process more daunting. But that does not mean that you will not get your loan; it just means that it will take more work and perseverance.

When shopping for a mortgage, there are a few major things you need to be prepared for. Here are a few:

Mortgage Fees

Mortgages cost money; and not just in the interest paid for the amount borrowed. Depending on the type of loan you are taking out, there may be a variety of fees charged, which must be paid up front. They may include:

Arrangement Fees

Arrangement fees are a type of lender fee charged to applicants to help them secure the most competitive rates.

Broker Fees

When using a mortgage broker, be aware that he or she does charge a separate fee for his or her services.

PMI

Private Mortgage Insurance (PMI) is a monthly fee charged to mortgages with less than 20 percent equity. This helps cover costs, should the borrower default on the loan. A few things you need to know about PMI are:

- It can be paid up-front (1 percent of the total house cost) and added to your mortgage, which may be cheaper in the long run

- It can be canceled once you have at least 20 percent equity in your home

- It is required by almost every lender today

Appraisal Fees

Before a lender will release any mortgage funds, you will have to prove with a written appraisal that the property is worth what you say it is. Of course, you, as the borrower, are responsible for paying for the appraisal.

Other Mortgage Fees and Charges

There are a number of hidden account fees that some lenders charge mortgage borrowers to complete their loan. While this list is by no means complete — always check with your lender for a complete list of fees they charge — it can give you an idea of what fees may be charged:

- Certificate of interest paid
- Consent to charge borrower priority
- Consent to second charge
- Data protection act fee
- Deeds access
- Property insurance
- Duplicate statements
- Extend/reduce mortgage term
- Information request from title deeds
- Legal documentation approval charge
- Lender's reference charge
- Mortgage account illustration fee
- Mortgage discharge fee
- Mortgage product transfer fee
- Photocopies of documents/deeds
- Property insurance substitution charge
- Questionnaire charge
- Repayment basis charge
- Revaluation charge
- Sale of part security
- Tenancy consent
- Title conversion
- Arrears administrative charge (monthly)

When shopping for a mortgage, be sure to carefully consider all your options to ensure you get the best deal, and one that you can live with for the next 20 to 30 years. Taking on the responsibility of a house can be overwhelming, especially at such a critical time in your life. Take your time. Even if money is not an issue, the stress and responsibility of buying a home can be harder than you think, and you may benefit from waiting a few months (or even a year) before delving into such a big undertaking so soon after your divorce or the death of your beloved spouse.

Loan/Mortgage Terms to Know

Assets – Anything you owe that is worth something.

Bad Debt – An unpaid debt.

Balance Sheet – A financial statement listing a person's debt and assets.

Collateral – Assets pledged to secure the repayment of a loan.

Current Asset – Any asset that will be turned into cash within the next 12 months.

Current Liability – Any liability scheduled to be repaid within the next 12 months.

Debt – Money owed to creditors.

Debt Service – The amount owed in regular payments to cover your current debt.

Default – Failing to make credit payments owed.

Delinquent – An overdue or past due amount.

Equity – Any value amount on a property above and beyond what is owed on it.

Interim Financing – A short-term loan used to provide temporary financial relief until a more permanent financing solution can be found.

Line of Credit – A loan offered to a borrower that allows them to take all or part of the total amount at their discretion as the need for funds arise.

Loan Agreement – A written contract between a lender and a borrower, which outlines the entire loan agreement.

Promissory Note – Written contract between a borrower and a lender.

Term – The time it will take to pay off a loan.

CHAPTER 7

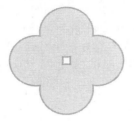

Getting Real — Learning to Live on One Income

When you have been used to living on more than one income, or maybe just more money, it can be a shock to try and squeeze your lifestyle into an income a fraction of the size you are accustomed to. No matter what the reason you are forced to cut back your expenses, it is not going to be easy. There will be emotional factors to deal with as you face the realities of your financial situation.

Maybe you feel guilty because your children must now attend public schools, or because they are forced to drop out of their favorite extracurricular activities. Or maybe you simply feel overwhelmed by the limitations your new income is placing on your spending and your inability to handle these changes. You are not alone.

It does not matter whether you are forced to scale back because you cannot make ends meet on your salary or because your spouse's Social Security will not stretch far enough. Change is in the air, and you will all need to learn to adapt, at least for a while. Things may not always be this tight, but for now they are, and every member of the family needs to face this reality to survive. Only then will you find a way to thrive once again.

Step No. 1: Take Stock of Your Bills

Your first order of business is to take stock of all your bills, make a list of everything you owe, and see where that list leads you. Maybe you will discover that your current income is enough to handle these expenses – most likely, you will discover that it is not. If your case is the latter, then it may be necessary to make some hard choices.

Step No. 2: Coming to Terms With Your New Financial Reality

Sometimes, couples think that it will be cheaper to live apart, but most American families struggle to survive on even two incomes.

Divorcing couples soon realize that it is cheaper to remain married. As a couple, you can work together to pay for one house, one set of living expenses, one vacation, and more. Apart, all those expenses double. Worse yet, you both may be socked with higher taxes as singles (thus making even less income), and many of the expenses that you pay jointly will rise when apart. Here are just a few of the expenses that will increase after your divorce:

- Two home payments (either rent or a mortgage)
- Two utility bills
- New furniture for the second household
- More convenience foods (singles are apt to spend more on these types of items)
- Two holiday expenses (most divorced couples each buy the children gifts)

Some individual expenses may go down after a separation, but not many, causing both spouses to feel the financial pinch after a divorce.

Widows and widowers, too, must face the reality of their new financial situation. Even if the surviving spouse always worked outside the home, their income is likely to diminish without the other's paycheck. This can be an even harder reality to handle because the family must also deal with the emotional impact of the death. While divorcing couples may have to face emotional turmoil themselves and with their children, they still have another person to help out in an emergency; the widow or widower does not.

The best thing anyone going through either of these scenarios can do right away is face his or her financial reality. As heartbreaking as it may be, do not try and keep your home if you know you cannot possibly afford it. Forget vacation and special outings for a few months until you figure out where you stand financially. You may even opt to pull the children (and yourself) out of any extracurricular activity that incurs a regular cost for the time being. That does not mean that you cannot enjoy your previous lifestyle again. But there must be a time of re-evaluation to see what you can afford, before you find yourself in serious financial ruin.

Step No. 3: Get Help

You do not have to figure this all out on your own. There are plenty of professionals out there willing to help you redesign your standard of living and budget to better match your new income. Make an appointment with a certified financial planner and/or accountant to see what your options are before making any drastic changes or decisions. Maybe you will be lucky and discover that things are not as bleak as they first appeared.

Step No. 4: Attack Your Bills One at a Time

When faced with more bills than you can pay, the next step is to attack those bills one at a time. Consider whether you need the item or service, and how you may be able to lower those monthly payments. Chipping away a little at a time may help you find the money you need without making any big changes, like selling your home or sending your children back to public schools. Look at your biggest bills first, asking yourself what changes can be made:

- **Mortgage:** If your mortgage is too high, you may have several options. You could try and refinance into a longer-term loan (or a lower interest rate) to lower payments, or you could consider renting out a spare room, garage, or basement to generate income. Of course, selling your home is also an option, but one that you should consider carefully — at least until you are sure that there is no other solution to your money woes.

- **Utilities:** There are many ways to cut back on your utility bills, starting with simply shutting off lights and appliances when not in use. Consider what eats into your utility budget the most, such as air conditioning, running the dryer, and wasted power. Find ways to cut back. Hanging your clothes on the line can cut your utility bills by $100 or more every month. So can lowering the heater on your hot tub (if it is kept outside). It may seem drastic to drain your pool or hot tub for a season, or to let your grass get a little dry by not watering it on a regular basis, but if it means staying in your home, it may be worth it.

- **Food:** Food costs are on the rise, and now is a good time to learn how to cut costs. Some major ways to trim your food costs are to avoid take-out, eat at home instead, pack lunches for both you and the kids, avoid prepackaged items, use coupons, and stock up during sales.

- **Children:** Children are expensive. They need new clothes, sports fees, books, school supplies, and many other things replaced on a regular basis. But that does not mean that you cannot find ways to trim their expenses, too. Some simple ways to cut your family budget when the need arises are to buy used toys and clothes, cut back on lessons and clubs, join free clubs at your local church or community center, and avoid high-priced amusements, going to the park instead. Learn more cost-cutting ideas in the next chapter.

- **Vacations and Fun:** Just because money is tight does not mean that you cannot take your children on a nice trip. You may just have to be a bit more creative now. Consider swapping homes with a faraway friend or relative, or staying in a rented cabin in the woods instead of a high-priced resort. There are plenty of ways to enjoy time away without spending thousands each year.

Another option for cutting your bills is to get rid of some of your debt. This may mean consolidating loans, paying off credit cards, negotiating lower rates with lenders, selling your car, downsizing your home, or giving up fancy vacations and some of the activities and things that you have become accustomed to. Simplifying your life and your bills is not going to be easy, but taking a realistic look at your needs is a good place to start.

In short, heading off financial trouble by accepting the reality of your new situation requires several things:

1. Negotiating a good divorce settlement.

2. Readjusting your spending so you do not have to tap into your other assets or your spouse's life insurance settlement for daily expenses.

3. Taking responsibility for your own financial well-being. This may require making big changes in the way you live, or even getting a job.

4. Accepting the new life ahead. You may have always had a membership at the local pool, or your children may have always taken private music lessons. If that is no longer the case, accept that. Your reality has changed, and so must your lifestyle. Be positive and show a good example to your children to help everyone better handle the changes ahead.

5. Being honest with your children. You cannot expect them to suddenly change yet one more thing in their lives without a good explanation. While it is not necessary or advisable to give them the

scary statistics, you should be as honest as you can about how your financial life has changed, and the ways you plan to adjust your lifestyle to meet it.

Determining Your True Worth

Those individuals who find themselves suddenly single again experience financial setbacks — or, worse, too little income to sustain their current lifestyle. Now that you have taken a hard look at your new income level and figured out how to best live on it — no matter what the size — it is time to look beyond your current financial state toward the future.

It can be difficult to move forward financially as a single person if you have no idea what you are worth. At first glance, you may think that you cannot survive today, let alone plan for a comfortable future. After all, it is hard to look beyond the here-and-now and see the big picture when you are struggling to get through today, emotionally and financially. But there is good news: Most people are worth much more than you think.

Getting a grasp on your net worth is an important factor to determining what you can afford now, and how you will manage down the line. Certainly, your financial picture has changed, but that does not mean that you will not have the money you need for your future. You may have it now and just not realize it.

While your day-to-day expenses should be covered by your current income, which will include any Social Security benefits, salaries, alimony, child support, or investment income, one thing to avoid at all costs is using your main assets to live on now. This is money that you will need for your future.

These assets may include such things as:

- **Property.** From your primary residence to a vacation home or even a business, property is a good investment in the future. In a divorce situation, you may lose some of your current property assets to your ex-spouse, but you should try and keep as much debt-free property assets as possible. Even if you decide that you cannot afford to keep that vacation property for yourself, you can either rent or sell it down the line and invest that money.

- **Retirement Monies.** In the event of your spouse's death, you will likely inherit any retirement monies that have been accumulated. Realize that these are assets to be used to safeguard your future. For those who are getting a divorce, do not overlook the possibility of being awarded a portion of your spouse's retirement accounts, especially if you do not have any retirement monies of your own saved prior to your divorce.

- **Savings.** The sad fact is that many new singles must use any cash savings to pay the bills until they figure out how to live on their new income. The key here is to try and keep as much as you can to use for investments and emergencies.

- **Business Profits.** If your spouse owned his or her own business, you are entitled to a portion of the business assets/profits following a divorce, and, most likely, most of them (if not all) after he or she has died. These are assets that must be handled carefully to ensure that you can sustain your current lifestyle now and in the years to come.

- **Insurance.** If you have been awarded any type of life insurance monies following the death of your spouse, you may be tempted to use it to pay your monthly bills. While this may be a necessity for some widows/widowers, remember that this money was meant to sustain your family over a long period of time and should be used sparingly, if possible.

In addition to these main assets, there are some easy-to-forget assets that should not be overlooked when determining your true worth:

- **Stock Options.** When negotiating a divorce settlement, do not overlook any stock options held by your spouse because they can be worth a bundle in the future. For those whose spouse has died, do not forget that you are now the rightful owner of these stock options and can legally buy, sell, or trade them in accordance with the law.

- **Tax Refunds.** If you and your spouse have filed a joint tax return, any refunds due will come in both of your names and should be dispersed accordingly.

- **Property Taxes.** In some cases, property taxes are paid in advance, leaving the spouse who gets the house a few months of free taxes. You may want to consider this when negotiating other aspects of your divorce settlement.

- **Frequent Flyer Points.** When a spouse dies, his or her frequent flier miles become part of his or her estate and are awarded to the surviving spouse — but when a couple divorces, those miles must be split amicably.

- **Season Tickets.** Again, all assets owned by a deceased spouse will be inherited by the surviving spouse in accordance with the legal will, but divorcing spouses must consider this type of asset when disbursing property equitably.

Looking for Hidden Assets:

Finding assets of a deceased spouse is straightforward, but that is not necessarily the case for those going through a divorce. Because every asset can be important when splitting property and determining future alimony and/or child custody payments, it is important to be sure that your ex-spouse is not hiding any assets from the lawyers and/or judge involved.

Here are a few common ways in which a spouse may try to either undervalue or hide marital assets:

- Collusion to delay work bonuses, stock options, or pay raises until after the divorce.
- Salary paid to a non-existent employee. Some self-employed individuals try this tactic as a way to lower their profit margin, only to cancel the checks after the divorce, leaving them with thousands in extra cash.
- A custodial account set up in the child's name. Although this may look like a good idea, it allows the parent who set up the account full access to the money before and after the divorce, leaving no guarantee that the child will ever receive the account in the future.
- Debt repayment to a relative or friend for a phony debt.
- Collections, antiques, or artwork that is undervalued and/or overlooked.

Once you have listed all your long-term assets, you will have a better idea of what you are truly worth. This should help give you at least some peace of mind that you cannot only survive — but can thrive — financially in the future.

CHAPTER 8

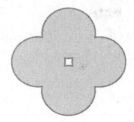

Savings Solutions — Simple Ways to Save Money

F inances can be tight after a major life-changing event, such as a divorce or a death in the family. Whether you are trying to make your life insurance premium or your child support stretch, or you simply want to find some extra money to save for the future, odds are that there are some ways to tighten your belt and free up some of your family cash flow.

Before offering ways for you to save and invest your money in the coming chapters, look at a few simple ways to find some extra dollars in the first place.

Quick Cash

No matter how tight you think your current budget is, there are likely a few ways you can generate some quick cash in an emergency. Here are a few to consider:

- **Trade in Your Vacation Days for Cash.** If you work full-time, and your employer is agreeable, you may be able to trade in some of your unused vacation days for real money in your paycheck.

- **Work Over-Time.** Not necessarily an option for a salaried employee, but hourly ones may be able to work some extra hours for some extra cash.

- **Call in Monies Owed.** If you have lent money to anyone in the past, call in those debts.

- **Refinance Your Home.** If you own your home and have the ability to refinance, you may be able to either lower your existing payments — giving you a few extra dollars every month — or use some of your equity to pay off other debt and free those payments.

- **Sell or Downgrade Your Car.** The average person spends more than $7,000 each year on their car payments, insurance, and maintenance. It is possible to cut that amount by two-thirds simply by getting rid of a newer car for an older model.

- **Sell Your Unwanted Items.** Everyone has hidden treasures lurking in their closets. Take whatever you can to the local consignment shop or list it online (**www.amazon.com**, **www.ebay.com**, and **www.craigslist.com** are three online markets people use often). You may be surprised at what it is worth.

Cutting Your Current Bills

To cut your current bills, try some of these cost-cutting measures:

- **Cut Back on Your Driving.** Today's gas prices can cut into a tight budget. The best way to save big on gas is to cut your consumption. Using public transportation or carpooling just two times per week can cut your total gas bill one-third every month. Some other simple ways to trim your gas bill include: doing all of your errands at one time instead of when individual needs arise; walking or bicycling whenever you can; and cutting back on your children's extracurricular activities to save on driving. Once you start thinking about how much it costs to drive somewhere, you may be amazed at how often you choose not to.

- **Buy Used.** There is little that you cannot buy used. From clothes, appliances, and books to cars, furniture, and toys, buying used can save the average consumer thousands every year.

- **Throw Out Those Catalogs.** Do not even look at a new catalog or sales ad unless you need something specific. The best way to save money is to not spend it in the first place.

- **Stay Home.** Eat in. Watch movies. Invite friends over for a fun night of games. Learning to enjoy simple activities at home can save you thousands in restaurant meals, movie tickets, and more.

- **Go Veggie.** Cook just three meatless meals per week and save more than $1,500 on groceries in just a year. It is a simple change — and healthy, too.

- **Save all Windfalls.** Got a tax refund this year? Won $10 on the lottery ticket your sister gave you for your birthday? Received a rebate in the mail? Put any windfall money directly into your emergency fund.

- **Raise Your Insurance Deductibles.** Unless you make many insurance claims, you are probably wasting several hundred dollars every year on low deductibles. Simply changing your deductible from $200 to $800 can save you hundreds in annual premium costs.

- **Avoid Unnecessary Fees.** Once you begin to look at all the convenience fees you may be accruing (e.g., ATM fees, monthly service charges, and unused service fees), you may be surprised at how much money you could save by streamlining your services. For instance, many stations charge as much as 10 cents more for each gallon of gas pumped if you pay with a credit card versus cash. That is just one example of how consumers pay for convenience.

- **Clean it Yourself.** Just because a label says "dry clean only" does not always mean it must be dry-cleaned — it just means that the manufacturer recommends that it be dry-cleaned. There are also home dry-cleaning products on the market. Try these to see if you can skip taking your clothes to a dry cleaner's.

- **Never Pay Full Price.** Most everything goes on sale eventually. Learn to wait to buy an item until it does.

Cutting your monthly living costs does not necessarily mean living like a pauper; it means looking closely at what you spend and how you may be wasting money on unnecessary objects and services.

If you are ready to go beyond these generic cost-cutters, try some of these more specialized savings options:

Utility Savings

- **Install a Digital Thermostat.** They are more accurate and allow you to better control the temperature in your home throughout the day. *Projected savings: 1 to 3 percent.*

- **Lower Your Heat.** Adjusting your thermostat just 2 degrees can save the homeowner on their monthly heating bill; the same is true for air conditioning costs. *Projected savings: 5 percent.*

- **Switch to Fluorescent Light Bulbs.** This switch will make your lights more energy-efficient and long-lasting. *Projected savings: 40 cents per bulb per month by making this simple switch.*

- **Open the Windows.** Creating a cross draft may eliminate the need for artificial cooling in some areas. *Projected savings: as much as $300 a month during peak summer seasons.*

- **Unplug Your Appliances.** Appliances can continue to use electricity, even when they are not in use — unless they are unplugged, that is. *Projected Savings: $1 to $5 per month.*

- **Wash in Cold Water.** Wash your clothes in cold water and save on your electric bill. *Projected savings: 10 percent.*

- **Ask For a Home Energy Audit.** Find out where you are losing heat and cooler air, and save hundreds of dollars every year. A simple call to your gas or electric company can result in a free energy audit designed to show you where problem areas are in your home. *Projected savings: more than $1,000 a year in home energy costs.*

- **Enroll in an Energy Management Program.** Most utility companies offer some sort of off-peak energy programs to help lower costs. *Projected savings: between $10 and $100 every month.*

- **Convert to a Gas Water Heater.** They are more energy-efficient and will cut your utility costs. *Projected savings: $1 to $50 per month.*

- **Shut the Vents in Unused Rooms.** Stop heating and cooling those rooms that you rarely use. *Projected savings: up to 25 percent on your monthly utility bills.*

Food Savings

- **Join a Food Co-op.** It will allow you to benefit from discount prices without buying in bulk. *Projected savings: 5 to 50 percent.*

- **Get Rain Checks.** When you find a good buy at the grocery store, wait until the last minute to get to the store. Chances are they will be out of the item, and you can get a rain check for it instead. This will allow you to enjoy the savings later when you need the item, without the need to stock up now. This buying strategy is especially good for perishable foods. *Projected savings: unlimited.*

- **Make Leftover-Friendly Meals**. Soups and casseroles both heat up and freeze well. *Projected savings: $2 to $5 per meal.*

- **Buy 2-liter Bottles of Soda Instead of Cans.** They are cheaper by unit. *Projected savings: $2 per bottle.*

- **Dig for Meat Choices.** Most butchers put the most expensive cuts of meat on the top of the pile in the meat case. Dig down a bit to find the real meat buys. *Projected savings: unlimited.*

- **Find a Day-Old Bakery.** Most bakery manufacturers have outlet stores, which offer merchandise at a reduced rate. *Projected savings: 20 to 70 percent.*

- **Beat the Clock.** There is a savings game played at pizza parlors all over the nation called Beat the Clock: A local pizza joint chooses a slow day and offers a large, plain pizza for the price of the time you called to order, between the hours of 3 p.m. and 6 p.m. Therefore, if you call in at 3:05, you get your pizza for $3.05. Because it is not always easy to get through right away, you may want to order several when you do get a good deal, and freeze the extras for another evening. *Projected savings: $3 to $9 per pie.*

- **Buy Pizza Dough.** Ask your local merchant whether he or she will sell you a container of ready-made dough, then make your own pizza pie at home. It is fun and tastes as good as restaurant-bought. *Projected savings: $3 to $5 per pie.*

- **Buy Foods From Organizations.** If you belong to a church, private school, or some other type of club or organization that may purchase food at wholesale prices, see whether you can place an order of your own using their discount. *Projected savings: 5 to 60 percent.*

- **Eat In-Season.** Eat only fresh fruits and veggies that are in-season — it is much cheaper. *Projected savings: 50 to 75 percent.*

- .**Buy Extra During Holiday Sales.** Turkeys are cheaper at Thanksgiving, as is ham at Easter. When you find a good holiday sale, buy extra and stock up. Meat can be frozen; baking goods can be stored in a pantry. *Projected savings: 20 to 50 percent.*

- **Ask For Gift Cards.** A good way to cut your food costs is to ask for grocery store gift cards from friends and family at the holidays. *Projected savings: unlimited.*

Saving on Children's Costs

- **Take Advantage of Free Classes.** From dance to karate, many sports and activity places offer one to four free introductory classes to get your children hooked on their service. Use these trial offers to introduce your children to new activities — even for a short period of time. *Projected savings: $25 to $100 a month.*

- **Check Out the Parks and Recreation Department.** Most municipalities offer loads of sports, activities, and classes at deep discounts. Handled by qualified professionals, these programs are often just as good as — if not better than — private classes. *Projected savings: 25 to 75 percent.*

- **Take Group Lessons.** Most music and dance teachers offer both private and group lessons. Of course, the group lessons are cheaper. *Projected savings: $5 to $20 per lesson.*

- **Cash in All of Those Free Photo Coupons.** Instead of paying the high price of school and sports photos, take advantage of those free photo offers you keep getting in the mail. They feature a free sitting fee and one large photo at no additional cost. *Projected savings: $12 to $25 per photo.*

- **Institute a Family Game Night.** Avoid the high price of going out together. Pull out those games crammed in your closet instead and have some good, old-fashioned fun. *Projected savings: $20 to $100.*

- **Limit Extracurricular Activities.** You do not have to make your children quit their favorite activities to save money, but you may need to limit them. *Projected savings: $25 to $200 per month.*

- **Sibling Discounts.** Whenever you have more than one child registered for an activity or class, be sure to check for any sibling discounts. *Projected savings: unlimited.*

- **Go Outlet Shopping.** To get name-brand merchandise for 30 to 80 percent off, hit the outlets. Check their clearance racks for even deeper discounts. *Projected savings: 30 to 80 percent off retail.*

- **Send in School Snacks and Drinks.** It may be easier to buy your children's snacks and drinks at school, but it is also more expensive. Pack them instead. *Projected savings: $1 to $2 per day per child.*

- **Take Your Own Sports Pictures.** With today's high-quality digital cameras and online photo accessory sites, it is easier than ever to take your own sports photos and have reprints made at your local photo-processing center, including those unique gift items. *Projected savings: $10 to $100 per child.*

- **Stay Away From Character Gear.** Buy more generic children's backpacks and lunch boxes that they can use for years. Character ones get outgrown much too soon. *Projected savings: 25 to 50 percent.*

Health and Beauty

- **Buy Prescriptions Through Mail Order.** Many insurance companies offer deep discounts if you purchase your medications through the mail. The most popular are the three-for-two offers, which allow you to purchase three months' worth of maintenance medications for only a two-month co-pay. *Projected savings: $5 to $50 per month for each prescription filled.*

- **Use generics.** Unless your doctor orders otherwise, they are just as good, and much cheaper. *Projected savings: $3 to $100 per medication.*

- **Stop Smoking.** Not only healthier for your body, it is healthier for your wallet. *Projected savings: $3 to $10 per day.*

- **Ask for Samples.** When starting a new medication, always ask the doctor for at least a week's worth of samples to avoid paying high co-pays on the full prescription until you are sure you can tolerate the new drug. *Projected savings: $10 to $100 per month.*

- **Call the Manufacturer For Help.** If you are finding it difficult to pay for high-priced medicines, call the pharmaceutical company that makes it and ask for help. Most have special programs that offer free or discounted medications to those who need it. *Projected savings: unlimited.*

- **Watch For Two-For-One Eyeglass Specials.** Most eye doctors are happy to give their patients a copy of their eyeglass prescription, which allows you to purchase your glasses at virtually any discount eyewear center. In addition, you can save even more by watching for those "buy one pair, get the second pair free" deals or "two pairs for $99" specials. Always ask whether both pairs of glasses must feature the same prescriptions. Most people assume that is the case, when in reality you can purchase two different prescription eyeglasses (one for you and one for someone else in your family) using the discount special. *Projected savings: $50 to $300.*

- **Use Baking Soda For Toothpaste.** It is clean and cheap. Mix a small amount of baking soda with water to create a paste-like mixture. *Projected savings: $3 per tube.*

- **Go to the Dentist at Your Local Dental School.** If you are not squeamish about letting a student care for your dental needs, you could save hundreds of dollars on check-ups and procedures. *Projected savings: 30 to 100 percent.*

- **Use Your Local Park's Playground Equipment as Your Fitness Center.** Monkey bars can be used for pull-ups and leg lifts, park trails are better than a treadmill, and stairs can be used in place of a Stairmaster machine. *Projected savings: $20 to $75 per month.*

- **Join Month-to-Month Gyms.** When choosing a fitness center, choose one that offers a month-to-month contract that you can cancel at any time without penalty, should you stop going for any reasons. *Projected savings: $30 to $75 per month.*

- **Head to the Local Beauty School.** Most beauty schools offer free or low-cost services to people who are willing to allow a student to practice on them. *Projected savings: 50 to 100 percent.*

Insurance Savers

- **Use the Same Carrier For All Your Policies.** Take advantage of multi-policy discounts. *Projected savings: 10 to 50 percent.*

- **Take Advantage of Good Student Discounts.** If you have a young driver in the house, insist on good grades to keep his or her driving privileges, then take advantage of any good student discounts offered by your insurance carrier. *Projected savings: 5 to 20 percent.*

- **Increase Your Deductible.** The higher your insurance deductible is, the lower your premium should be. *Projected savings: 5 to 30 percent.*

- **Get Rid of Your Private Mortgage Insurance (PMI).** If you have at least 20 percent equity in your home, get rid of the PMI. It will save you 1 percent of your total mortgage cost each month.

- **Pay Insurance Bills Annually.** By paying your premiums annually, you may qualify for up to 10 percent off.

- **Drop the Benefits You do Not Need.** Some health care providers will allow you to drop the benefits that you do not need for a discount. For instance, if your child-bearing years are over, whether due to age or a surgical procedure, you may be able to drop the maternity on your family policy and save. *Projected savings: 5 to 30 percent.*

Family Fun

- **Swap Houses.** If you have friends or acquaintances who live far away or near an attraction that you would like to visit, try swapping houses for your next vacation: They stay at yours while you stay at theirs. It is a good way to take a vacation and save money on hotels and restaurants. *Projected savings: $500, $3,000 — or more.*

- **Buy Tickets and Accommodations at Fundraising Auctions.** All kinds of schools, clubs, churches, sports teams, and community groups have charity auctions every year where many new and used items are sold at a fraction of their original cost — including vacation packages and timeshare accommodations. It is not uncommon for bidders to walk away from one of these sales with a weeklong stay at a nice resort for 50 to 90 percent off the retail value. *Projected savings: $100 to $5,000.*

- **Join Away From Home.** If your family loves museums, zoos, and aquariums, then consider purchasing a family museum membership, but not at your local attraction — choose one farther from home. When you join a museum or zoo with a reciprocating membership to the ones near your own home, you can visit both for free. There is one important rule, though: You can only visit ones at least 90 miles away from the one you purchased it at, so be sure to choose your membership carefully. *Projected savings: $25 to $90 per membership.*

- **Be Spontaneous.** One good thing about being single again is that you can often be more spontaneous, and that can mean big travel savings. People who are able to drop everything and head to the airport on a moment's notice can benefit from high savings by taking advantage of open airline seats and canceled hotel reservations. *Projected savings: 25 to 75 percent.*

- **Book Airline Tickets and Hotels Months in Advance.** When you purchase tickets and book hotel stays far in advance, it can cost much less. *Projected savings: 5 to 45 percent.*

- **Avoid Renting a Car at the Airport.** Take a taxi or shuttle to a car rental agency a few blocks from the airport and get a more competitive rate, plus avoid extra surcharges. *Projected savings: $3 to $20 per rental.*

- **Travel Off-Season.** Traveling during the off-season is easier and cheaper. Plus, there are fewer crowds. *Projected savings: 25 to 80 percent.*

- **Rent a Friend's Timeshare.** Many people own timeshares that they simply cannot use every year. Find someone who is willing to rent you his or her unused one for the cost of his or her annual fees. *Projected savings: $200 to $2,000 per week.*

- **Order Children's Meals.** When grabbing take-out at a park or attraction, consider ordering children's meals for everyone. They are good for lunches on-the-go and come complete with an entrée, sides, drink, and even dessert for half the price of a full-sized meal. *Projected savings: $1.50 to $5.00 per meal.*

- **Take Along Your Own Drinks.** Most attractions and amusement parks now allow you to bring in your own snacks and drinks. This can be a big cost saver. *Projected savings: $2 to $36 per day.*

- **Use Club Memberships for Discounts.** If you belong to AAA or AARP, chances are, they offer discounts on hotel stays, restaurant meals, and car rentals, among others. Always ask to see whether a discount may apply. *Projected savings: unlimited.*

- **Buy Your Tickets Before Leaving Home.** Many municipalities now offer discount amusement tickets at their main office. *Projected savings: 5 to 50 percent.*

- **Plan a Group Trip With Friends, Family, or Neighbors.** Plan your next outing with another family or two, and take advantage of group rates at most attractions. *Projected savings: 10 to 50 percent.*

- **Cook In.** Supply your own meals as much as possible when on vacation. Take along cereal for breakfast, pack a toaster, and make your own sandwiches for lunch. *Projected savings: 5 to 50 percent.*

- **Avoid High-Priced Restaurants.** If you do need to eat out, choose smaller, family-owned restaurants, diners, and all-you-can eat buffets. *Projected savings: 5 to 50 percent.*

- **Visit Off-the-Beaten-Path Destinations.** To save the most money, stay away from high-priced tourist areas. Head for lesser-traveled areas instead. *Projected savings: 10 to 60 percent.*

- **Visit State Parks.** There is plenty to see and do for free at the nation's national parks. *Projected savings: unlimited.*

- **Visit Free Places.** Nearly every community in every part of the world has local museums and attractions that offer free admittance. Check those out first whenever away from home. *Projected savings: $2 to $30 per ticket.*

- **Attend Second-Run Movie Theaters**. If you are willing to wait until the end of a movie run to go see it, you can buy a ticket for as little as $1 at these cheap theaters. *Projected savings: $2 to $8 per ticket.*

Transportation

- **Ask Your Insurance Agent About a Multi-Car Discount.** Many insurance companies offer discounted rates for multiple cars within the same family. *Projected savings: 5 to 10 percent.*

- **Buy Used.** A used car costs less, and so does the insurance. *Projected savings: $50 to $400 a month.*

- **Lower Insurance.** Many insurance carriers use your credit score to determine your insurance premiums. Keep your credit in good standing, and enjoy cheaper insurance. *Projected savings: 5 to 20 percent.*

- **Keep Your Tires Inflated.** Keep the tires inflated properly and save. *Projected savings: 3 to 5 percent.*

- **Keep Your Vehicle Well-Maintained.** Cars that are not maintained properly are less fuel-efficient. *Projected savings: 2 to 10 percent.*

- **Remain Accident-Free.** The longer you can drive without filing a claim with your insurance carrier, the cheaper your premiums will be. *Projected savings: 5 to 25 percent.*

- **Drive Fewer Miles.** In many states, there are big benefits to driving less. For instance, in Pennsylvania, vehicles that register less than 5,000 miles a year for two years or more are exempt from high-priced emissions testing and regulations, get a discount on tags and registration fees, and enjoy much cheaper insurance rates with most carriers. *Projected savings: $30 to $500 per year.*

- **Avoid carrying added weight in the trunk.** Having excess weight in the bed of your truck decreases your gas mileage. *Projected savings: $5 to $25 per month.*

- **Do not rest your foot on the clutch or brake.** Resting your foot on the brake or clutch can causes needless wear and poor fuel economy. *Projected savings: 2 to 8 percent.*

- **Keep Your Front Wheels in Proper Alignment.** Improper alignment causes faster wear on the tires and puts an extra load on the engine. *Projected savings: unknown.*

- **Rotate Your Tires Regularly.** Rotating tires on your vehicle on a regular basis prevents tire wear. *Projected savings: 3 to 5 percent.*

Banking

- **Use Your Credit Card for More Purchases if You Pay it Off Each Month.** Using your credit card to make purchases will enable you to rack up those bonus points and cash back points fast, but you must pay it off completely every month. *Projected savings: unlimited.*

- **Open an Online Savings Account.** They usually offer at least 1 percent higher interest rate than standard accounts. *Projected savings: 1 percent of your balance.*

- **Avoid Using the ATM.** They feature high fees. *Projected savings: $1 to $100 per month.*

- **Pay Bills by Direct Debit.** Not only will you save postage costs, but you will not have to pay any more late fees. *Projected savings: unlimited.*

- **Buy Your Checks Through the Mail.** Banks charge a large amount for check printing. Order them through the mail or online instead. *Projected savings: 10 to 50 percent.*

- **Use an Online Broker.** Avoid high commission rates by using cheaper brokerage companies online. *Projected fees: 5 to 30 percent.*

- **Combine Accounts.** Avoid many account fees by combining accounts at one bank. *Projected savings: $5 to $100 per month.*

- **Keep Extra Money in High-Yield Accounts.** You can earn big dividends. *Projected savings: 3 to 15 percent.*

Miscellaneous

- **Never Turn Away a Freebie.** Even if you cannot use a specific free-bie right now, throw it in a box and use as a gift, or sell it online or at a yard sale. Better yet, donate the items to a charity and claim the tax deduction on your income taxes. *Projected savings: unlimited.*

- **Go Digital.** Stop paying for film and developing. Go digital and only print out the pictures that you want to keep. *Projected savings: $5 to $50 per month.*

- **Host a Party for Free Merchandise.** From make-up and home decorative items to food and craft supplies, there are many home party products out there that can be yours simply by hosting an in-home demonstration. *Projected savings: $20 to $300.*

- **Relocate.** If you live in a high-priced area of the country, consider relocating to a cheaper place to live. *Projected savings: unlimited.*

- **Buy Your Own Exercise Equipment.** With the high cost of a gym membership these days, you can buy used exercise equipment for only one to three months' worth of membership fees. *Projected savings: $3 to $75 per month.*

- **Use the Library.** Borrow books, videos, and magazines from the local library. *Projected cost: unlimited.*

- **Trade Your Craft Supplies.** Instead of buying new products, have a craft swap with your buddies featuring everyone's unused items for trade. *Projected savings: unlimited.*

- **Order Single Songs, not Albums.** Unless you listen to every song on an album, only buy the singles you like most from your favorite music downloads sites. *Projected savings: $1 to $15 per album.*

- **Grow Your Own Flowers.** If you like fresh-cut herbs and flowers, consider growing your own. *Projected savings: unlimited.*

Holidays and Gifts

- **Buy Gifts Year-Round.** Do not wait until the last minute to buy holiday gifts — it may cost you more. Watch those sales and clearance racks during the year to find just the right gifts at a fraction of their original cost. *Projected savings: 10 to 90 percent.*

- **Use Comics for Wrapping Paper.** It is an inexpensive wrapping paper. *Projected savings: $5 to $50 per year.*

- **Purchase a Real Tree a Few Days Before Christmas.** If you do not mind putting your Christmas tree up a few days (or even the day before) Christmas, you can find a wonderful tree for a fraction of the cost. *Projected savings: 50 to 75 percent.*

- **Frequent Church Bazaars.** Baking a variety of homemade holiday treats can be expensive and time-consuming. Most churches and retirement homes have holiday bazaars in December, featuring a wonderful variety of homemade cookies, cakes, pies, and more at a much lower price. *Projected savings: 20 to 75 percent.*

- **Host a Cookie Swap.** Why waste the money on ingredients for five different kinds of Christmas cookies? Get a few friends together and hold a cookie swap instead. It is fun and cost-efficient. *Projected savings: 10 to 50 percent.*

- **Bake Your Own Birthday Cakes.** Take a cake-decorating class and save by foregoing those fancy store-bought cakes. *Projected savings: $10 to $30 per cake.*

- **Let Your Children Make Decorations.** Children love to decorate. Get out their craft supplies and let them make their own party decorations. *Projected savings: unlimited.*

- **Make Your Own Cards.** Card-making is becoming popular these days, and is much less expensive than buying ones in the store. *Projected savings: $0.50 to $5 per card.*

- **Send E-mail Cards.** Cut the cost of buying holiday cards and postage by sending free e-mail greetings and cards. *Projected savings: $0.50 to $3 per card.*

- **Send Postcards Instead.** Cut your postage bill in half by sending holiday postcards. *Projected savings: $0.20 per card.*

- **Make Your Own All-Occasion Wrapping Paper.** Use your children's artwork or leftover scraps of material to wrap small gifts. *Projected savings: unlimited.*

- **Cook an Extra Large Turkey or Ham.** Freeze the leftovers for meals throughout the winter. *Projected savings: $5 to $7 per meal.*

- **Offer a gift service.** Give family and friends your time as a gift like free babysitting, lawn care, or even house cleaning. It costs you nothing, but your time of course, and may be more appreciated than a "bought" gift. *Projected savings: unlimited.*

Know When to Shop for Bargains:

Savvy shoppers know that eventually everything goes on sale. But, what happens when you do not want to wait around for something specific to be discounted? You may have to. Certain manufacturers commonly offer their deepest discounts during specific months of the years.

As you can see, there are plenty of ways to save money. Some may look difficult, but if you adopt enough small changes, you may not have to consider the bigger changes that are harder for some families to handle.

CHAPTER 9

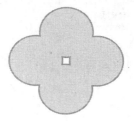

Managing Your Investments

For many new singles, the thought of how to best invest their assets may seem foreign — especially if they always left that part of their financial lives up to their spouses. If you are finding the mere thought of investing complicated, not to mention a bit daunting, then it is time that you learn a few of the basics.

Cash Assets

Not everyone has a portfolio of stocks, bonds, or other investments to rely on, especially after a life-altering event like a divorce or spousal death. For some, saving for the future may take a while, leaving their options more limited to cash-style investments. These include:

Passbook Savings

Once considered the only way to save, traditional passbook savings accounts have been passed over for higher-yield savings options by most. Still, being able to save what you can, earn a little interest, and still have instant access to your money in an emergency can be just what you need until you are back on your financial feet once again.

Money Market Deposit Accounts

Requiring at least $1,000 to open and maintain this type of account, a money market allows you to earn a higher interest rate by limiting the number of deposits/withdrawals you can make in any given month.

Money Market Mutual Funds

Unlike a strict money market deposit account, which works much like a standard savings account, a money market mutual fund is run by a fund management company, which decides how your money will be invested. Benefits include wide diversification, higher interest earned, and interest credited daily. However, no investment plan comes without some risk. Mutual funds are no exception, as they:

1. Are not insured by the FDIC.

2. Are subject to taxes in some cases — and, of course, profits earned are always taxable.

3. Feature limitations in accordance to the type of fund invested in.

Treasury Bills (T-Bills)

Treasury Bills, most commonly known as T-bills, are a skittish investor's dream, as they offer the most security for cash investments. Backed by the federal government, T-Bills offer a good return on your investment and are insured for safety. Treasury Bills are sold in increments above $10,000 and are held between 13 and 26 weeks. Of course, the longer you hold your T-Bill, the more money you will make. They can be purchased directly from the Federal Reserve, or from any bank for a $25 charge. Although income generated from a T-Bill is subject to federal income taxes, they are exempt from state and local taxation.

Certificates of Deposit (CDs)

Certificates of Deposit (CDs) are savings options offered by financial institutions such as banks and credit unions, which allow you to earn interest by committing your money to a three-, six-, nine-, or 12-month certificate of deposit. Some financial institutions even offer longer-term CDs for a higher yield. Of course, if you need your money before the certificate's maturity date, you will be subject to hefty penalties. Still, it is a wonderful way to save short-term and still make some profits.

Fixed Income Assets

Bonds

When you buy a bond, you are giving a company or municipality the money it needs to do something, like build a new facility or make some other lasting improvement. In return, the issuer promises to send you monthly or quarterly interest payments, as well as the money you invested, upon the bond's maturity.

A relatively safe way to invest, bonds not only help you (the investor) make money, but they help the company or government entity issuing the bond pay for important projects. Although they do not allow the purchaser to make the same fantastic gains as stocks may, they do offer a safe way to make some decent profits over a long period of time.

Bonds come in several different categories, or grades:

- AAA, AA, or A bonds offer virtually no risk, as they are backed by a highly profitable corporation or agency.
- BBB are medium-risk bonds, but still a relatively safe investment.
- Bonds lower than a BBB rating carry a much higher risk of default.
- Junk bonds offer the highest risk and are often worth nothing by the time they reach their maturity date.

Stocks

When you purchase stocks, you are purchasing ownership in a company. The number of shares you own, compared to the number of shares available, will determine how much equity you have in that company. Owning just a few shares will not give you much power in the day-to-day operations of a company, but it will enable you to make a bit of a profit should share prices begin to soar.

As investors have seen in recent months, stocks are best handled as a long-term investment, and can at times be risky when purchased with the hope of making short-term profits.

An investment in common stocks means buying a smaller stream of earnings over a period of time. The more reliable that stream of earnings is, and the more quickly it grows, the more investors are willing to pay for the stock, which in turn makes your investment more profitable.

There are three types of stocks for sale:

- **Large-Cap Stocks.** These are stocks from well-established companies with capitalization equaling more than $5 billion. They offer a large volume of trading and are easy to track. They offer little risk of company failure and pay regular dividends.

- **Small-Cap Stocks.** These stocks are offered by lesser-known companies and feature less than $1.5 billion in capitalization. They feature small and hard to trade volume, potentially big gains, and high risk, especially in regard to company failure and poor management.

- **Mid-Cap Stocks.** These are stocks offered by companies featuring $1.5 billion and $5 billion in capitulation, and they may offer fast-growth potential. They offer a large volume of trading and are easy to trade.

With so many options available, steps must be taken to know what stocks are best for you. The first thing you must do is determine the company's current value. This can be done by looking at:

1. Its history (has its stock gone up and down in price over the years, or stayed relatively stable?) Here are some questions to ask when looking more deeply into a company's history:

    a. Has the company's composition changed recently due to a merger, acquisition, or divestiture?

    b. Have there been any major managerial changes?

    c. Has its earning slowed? Why?

    d. What is going on in the economy? Will it affect this particular business or industry?

2. The value of their competitors over time.

3. The current value of the industry. Are there things happening within that specific industry that may cause its stock to rise or fall in value?

4. The market. What is the stock market itself doing these days?

When choosing a good stock to buy, be sure to measure its relative value in comparison to how strong the company stands financially. If you find a cheap stock, there may be a good reason. Unless you can be confident that you are not buying into a company that is poised for failure, stay clear — at least, until you learn how to play the stock market game better.

Factors to Consider When Investing in Mutual Funds:

Becoming increasingly popular, mutual funds are a way to expand or diversify your investment portfolio — thus making the most profit for the least amount of risk — by pooling your money with other investors to purchase higher-yield stocks, bonds, and cash equivalents. The rationale with this type of investment is that if one fund does poorly, another will negate the loss.

Although they can be a good way to ensure some investment success, there are still some important factors to consider when selecting a mutual fund:

- Know the basics.
- Develop an investment plan. Know your goals and timeline.
- Develop an investment strategy.
- Develop screening criteria.
- Watch performance levels. Always watch for investment trends over a several-year period.
- Understand the fund's risk profile or volatility.
- Focus on returns. Watch for funds that charge higher-than-average fees and taxes.
- Invest with the best. Know the manager.
- Research, research, research. Check out the funds you are considering on the Internet. Web sites such as **www.morningstar.com**, **www.mutualfundreporting.com**, **www.brill.com/fundlink.html**, **www.smartmoney.com**, **www.money.com**, and **www.CNNfn.com** all have extensive online information and data available for review.

Finding Your Investment Approach

There are many different ways to invest your money for the future, and which one you choose depends largely on your investment approach.

If you are skittish, or simply cannot afford to lose money, you may want to concentrate on a more conservative investment approach that consists of concentrating on liquidity, secure stock, and high-rated, fixed-growth investments. This is best accomplished by investing in shorter U.S. Treasury bond funds, money markets, CDs, high-rated municipal bonds, mutual funds, and longer maturity Treasury bonds. Although these types of investments offer low risk for investors, they are also quite limited in the amount of profits that can be generated.

A more moderate approach can give you higher returns with minimal risk and requires investing in high-rated corporate bonds and mutual funds, balanced stocks, Dow Jones and S&P 500 Index and Blue Chip stock mutual funds, and large and medium capitalization mutual funds.

If you are not afraid to risk your investment, you can enjoy larger profits by purchasing small capitalizations (NASDAQ) mutual funds; high yield or junk bonds; international bonds; sector mutual bonds in technology, health care, or another field; and individual common stocks.

High rollers with little to lose may opt for a more speculative approach, which offers the most risk, but also higher-than-average profits to be potentially gained. Featuring unpredictable results, speculative investments include futures options, speculative stocks, and venture capital.

While a low/limited risk approach to investing is the safest way to enter the investing world, keep in mind that the less risky an investment is, the less profit you will ultimately make. Some low-risk investments end up losing money in the long run, as they may not keep up with inflation, and the principle may be eaten away after paying taxes.

If you are not sure how best to invest your capital, consider this common breakdown that allows you to garner higher yields, while keeping some of your money safe:

- **Emergency:** 25 – 100 percent
- **Conservative:** 0 – 50 percent
- **Moderate:** 0 – 33 percent
- **High:** 0 – 15 percent
- **Speculative:** 0 – 10 percent

Tips to Developing and Managing Your Investment Portfolio

Diversify; the best portfolio contains a nice mixture of low, moderate, and maybe even a small amount of high-risk investments. Some factors to consider when building your investment portfolio include:

- **Liquidity** – How accessible is your money?
- **Safety** – How much risk are you assuming with your investment?
- **Return** – How much can you expect to make?
- **Tax Considerations**

When determining how to invest your spouse's retirement savings, insurance payoff, or even your divorce settlement, find the approach that best suits your needs and comfort level. Invest only as much as you are willing to lose, and remember, a conservative approach means investing in liquid investments, blue chip stocks, and high-rated, fixed-income investments. Moderate risk offers medium exposure to growth stocks, mutual funds, and bonds, while high-growth (and high-profit) investments usually mean risking your investment in speculative growth stocks.

Once you have measured your possible risk and ultimate reward, look at your personal views on investing before making any final decisions. This includes:

- Developing a game plan, and sticking to it.

    - Set up an investment account, and contribute to it monthly.
    - Actively pursue your investment goals.
    - Develop just the right mix of investments that allow you to meet your goals with minimal risk.
    - Stop spending. The easiest way to make a dollar is to not spend it.

- Knowing what you own and why you own it.

- Staying focused.

- Looking at dips in the market as opportunity for future growth and profits.

- Remembering that diversification is the key to success.

While being left with a sudden windfall to invest may seem complicated, it does not have to be. The key is to learn what best suits your needs and comfort, and find a professional who is willing to take the time to help you learn what you need to know about investing.

Understanding the Stock Market

The stock market is a confusing world. Constantly changing and evolving, it requires at least some knowledge of how it all works. A good place to start is to learn about these basic indexes:

The Dow Jones Industrial Average

The most popular of all the world's stock exchanges, it tracks 30 of the highest blue chip stocks traded on the New York Stock Exchange.

The NASDAQ Composite Index

An index that tracks any company on the NASDAQ

The Standard and Poor's 500 Index

The S&P 500 is the benchmark for investors. It comprises 500 blue chip stocks from a variety of industries, which allows investors to see what the overall stock market is doing at a glance.

All Other Indexes

Some other indexes you may hear about include:

- The New York Stock Exchange Composite Index
- The Wilshire 5,000 Equity Index
- A variety of foreign indexes, which tell you what the foreign investment market is doing

CHAPTER 10

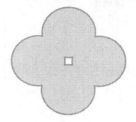

Ask Uncle Sam –
Understanding Your
New Tax Reality

Any time you have a major life change, it may have a drastic effect on your taxes. The death of your spouse or the end of your marriage through divorce is no exception. Couples save thousands of dollars every year in personal income taxes simply by filing jointly. Take away that option, and you may find yourself owing Uncle Sam more than you ever did before. But, before you begin to panic, wondering how in the world you will handle one more bill on your new income, let us address some of the new tax realities new widow(er)s and divorced individuals must face.

Your Taxes After a Spouse's Death

The bad news is that if your income level stays about the same (or is higher) after your spouse's death, you will likely be required to pay more in federal income taxes in the years to come. The good news is that increase will not go into effect for a few years.

Would it not be nice if the tax man took a break after the death of your spouse? Unfortunately, he does not, and in some cases may take a keener interest in your returns following a major life change such as widowhood.

In addition to dealing with your spouse's income taxes, you may also have to claim certain inheritances, capital gains, and other state and local taxes that you may know little, if anything, about. But first, concentrate on any federal taxes you may be required to pay.

Filing Your Spouse's Last Income Tax Return

You would think that once a person dies, he or she would not be required to pay any more taxes. Not true. The taxpayer's estate (namely you), are now responsible for settling up with Uncle Sam for any unpaid taxes due at the time of your spouse's untimely death.

There are several ways in which the Feds determine income for tax purposes following a death by taxing income on either:

- The taxpayer's final return

- The tax return of the beneficiary who acquires the right to receive the income

- The estate's income tax return if it has generated more than $600 in income during the year in question.

It is preferred that the deceased final return be filed by the executor of his/her estate, or if none is named, a survivor.

When filing this last tax return, be sure to use the same form that would have been used if the taxpayer were still alive, but write "deceased" after his/her name. The filing deadline is April 15 of the year following the taxpayer's death.

Determining Your Spouse's Income

When filing your deceased spouse's final tax return, you must include all income earned between the first of the year and the date of his or her death. For most, that will require finding pay stubs and income received during this time period. However, taxpayers who use an accrual method of accounting must report all earnings — no matter when they were received. This is important to consider because some income, which may at first seem like it should go on the deceased's final return, might be taxed as income charged to his/her survivors and/or estate.

When considering who is responsible for paying the taxes on certain income amounts, consider whether it was income that the deceased had a right to receive at the time of his or her death. For instance, interest earned after his or her death should not be included on the final return, but as part of the survivor's income instead. This can cause some headaches for those filing the returns because mutual funds, banks, and brokers may include this type of income on the deceased 1099 forms, even though it cannot be included as income on their tax return. The best way to avoid these types of problems is to have all investment accounts changed over into the new owner's name as soon as possible after the death.

DID YOU KNOW?

Money you inherit from a deceased spouse is not subject to the federal income tax, but the interest earned on it is. So, if your spouse leaves you a $100,000 certificate of deposit, that $100,000 is not taxable — only the interest you earn after it becomes yours is taxed.

There is a special rule for U.S. savings bonds, however, because they are not taxed until after they are cashed in. To avoid paying taxes on the entire profit generated from the bonds, it is possible for survivors to include interest earned up to the date of the deceased's death on their final tax return, thus only claiming the interest earned after the death on their own tax returns. This can be an especially smart, tax-saving move for low-income beneficiaries.

Determining Your Spouse's Deductions

Deductions are a bit easier to calculate than income because they are more straightforward. The biggest questions come in regard to the date of death and any medical bills accrued during the last year of the taxpayer's life.

The rule of thumb to go by in regard to your spouse's deductions is this: All deductible expenses paid before his/her death can be legally written off on the final return, including all medical bills paid within one year after his or her death, no matter when your spouse died. Even if the date of death is January 1 of the taxing year, you may claim all deductions in full on his or her last return. There is no need to prorate any deductions. The same is true for those who do not itemize deductions, but take the standard one instead. If deductions are not itemized on the final return, the full standard deduction may be claimed, regardless.

Determining Your Spouse's Filing Status

Not only can you legally file a joint tax return for the year in which your spouse died, but in most cases for the two consecutive years following his or her death, too. This will allow you to take advantage of any tax benefits you experienced as a married couple while still trying to figure out your new income limitations

When filing a joint return, the estate's executor or administrator signs the return for the deceased, and if no executor is appointed, then the surviving spouse may do it as long as he/she writes "on behalf of the decedent," or "filing as a surviving spouse," next to his or her signature.

In the event a refund is due, you must file one additional form to have it issued in your name alone: Form 1310, Statement of Person Claiming Refund Due a Deceased Taxpayer. The IRS does not say you have to file

Payments by a Spouse

Spouses making alimony payments may take a deduction for those payments, as long as they are paid in cash and ordered by your divorce decree, while those receiving these payments are required to pay taxes on this "income."

Do not confuse alimony payments with child support — child support payments are not taxed on the receiving end, and the payer does not receive any type of deduction for making them.

Asset Transfers

When you shift ownership of property from one spouse to another in a divorce settlement, it is important to consider the tax implications — now and in the future.

While you may not be required to pay any transfer taxes for property gained from a divorce settlement, you will be required to pay all capital gains from profits both before and after the divorce, should you ever sell it. This can make a big difference in the amount you think you receive from your divorce and the money you are left with.

Home Sales

If you decide to sell your home after a divorce, you may not have to pay as much in capital gains taxes as you first thought. Under the current law, couples are exempt from paying capital gains on the first $500,000 on property as long as they have lived in it two of the last five years. Those who are divorcing can each take half of that $500,000 amount toward their own tax criteria. If, however, you have lived in the home less than two years, you may be able to prorate the exemption, and then split it between the two of you.

Retirement Assets

Be careful how you distribute retirement savings during a divorce. For instance, if you cash out your 401(k) plan to buy out your spouse's interest in it, you will be hit with both taxes and penalties. The best way to avoid these extra costs is to transfer the monies using a qualified domestic relations order (QDRO). This will allow your spouse to take over the funds without causing your taxable income to rise. There are a lot of things to consider when filing your taxes after a divorce or death. The reality is that you will likely be paying more taxes now as a single person, even if your income is less than it was before. But understanding your rights and responsibilities can help you avoid costly mistakes when dealing with the IRS.

Who Gets to Claim the Children?

The tax implications of claiming your children as dependents on your tax returns can be huge, no matter what your current income level. With dependency exemptions ranging from $3,300 to nearly $8,000 per child, depending on whether you claim head of household, the need to fight for these exemptions is paramount for most parents.

While a parent who is paying high child support may feel that he or she is entitled to child exemptions, the law allows the custodial parent — the one caring for the children in his or her home — to take it, unless he or she signs a waiver (IRS Form 8332), giving the other parent permission to use the exemptions for himself or herself.

 While the law seems clear, trouble can arise when your ex decides to beat you to the punch and file his/her tax return first, claiming the exemption for his or her own. Once the IRS sees that two parents have used the child's Social Security number to claim the exemptions, it will up to the IRS auditor to determine who is in compliance with the law and who is not. The best thing to do when this situation occurs is to have your custody papers ready and any other proof that the child in question does reside with you. This might include school records and medical reports.

While it may be a hassle to prove who was right and who was wrong, keep in mind that a spouse who illegally claims a dependent on his or her income tax return will be subject to taxes, penalties, and fines once the situation is figured out during the audit phase.

Estimating Your New Take-Home Pay: Changing Your Form W-4

While you were married, you may have allowed your boss to withhold more taxes from your weekly earnings to enjoy a larger refund at year's end. But now that you are single again, you may need every penny. That is why it is so important to give Uncle Sam only the amount he needs to cover your annual tax bill — and no more.

To cover your taxes before they come due, employers are required to withhold a certain amount of each employee's paycheck for taxes. How much they keep back is determined by what you put on your W-4 Form, also referred to as the Employee's Withholding Allowance Certificate.

On this form, you will list whether you are married or single, how many dependents you have, and how many withholding allowances you can take. The more allowances you list, the less in taxes your employer will withhold from your paycheck.

Most people remember filling out a W-4 Form when they started a new job, but now that your life situation has changed, it is important to ask for a new form to ensure that you are both paying enough in taxes, and not paying too much. Some things to look for when deciding whether to re-file a W-4 Form is:

- receiving more than $1,00 a year in refund monies
- paying more than 10 percent of your monthly income in taxes

How to Change Your W-4 Withholding

To change your withholding tax, simply head to your employer's human resources office and ask for a new W-4 Form. Next, look at all of your allowances, including dependents, child care expenses, head of household status, and your tax write-offs for the year.

Most people fail to consider their tax write-offs when determining their withholding tax, only to be left paying in too much and cheating themselves out of money that could be used throughout the year to pay their monthly expenses. Of course, by paying in "just enough," you will eliminate any tax refunds in the spring. However, it is a great way to put more money in your pocket right now.

CHAPTER 11

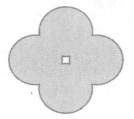

Understanding Child Support and Alimony

Alimony and child support can be nearly as emotional and difficult as custody issues when you and your former spouse are going through the divorce process. Emotions run high as finances come into play and you both attempt to rebuild a life split in two. Money is one of the biggest conflict-ridden topics within a marriage, and may even have been a factor leading to your divorce. Dividing a household financially, even under the best of circumstances, would be difficult, but with the added pressures of divorce and possibly unfriendly custody disputes, it can be fraught with hazards.

It is simple to say that support issues should be dealt with in a logical, im-partial, even detached manner, but nearly impossible to accomplish. If you are able to work out an agreement on your own, without court intervention, you may find the process smoother and less costly. Your agreements will still need to be documented by the courts for legal and taxation purposes, but the whole process may be best handled by you and your soon-to-be ex-spouse. If that seems impossible, you can use the resources and knowledge of the court system and your lawyers to sort out the financial maze that lies ahead for both of you.

Taking one household and making two will be costly for both parties. In addition to separate homes, there will be additional responsibilities and costs associated with living independently. Spousal and child support exist to help make the transition — and the subsequent lifestyle — look a bit more like what you have had before the divorce, but it is not a perfect system. Look at what spousal and child support will mean for your new family structure, what you need to know, and what you will want to remember as you begin to separate financially from your spouse.

Spousal support and child support share many common characteristics, but also differ in important ways. Spousal support may be ordered in the case of a divorce, and exists to help the receiving spouse try to maintain a way of life at least similar to the one enjoyed during the marriage. Child support, on the other hand, will always be ordered because parents have a legal (and ethical) obligation to support their children, whether or not those children live with them. Even if the amount one parent is able to pay is small, it will still be required.

You will find further similarities between spousal and child support, as well as important differences that must be noted if you are pursuing a judgment for either type.

Alimony

Most commonly known these days as spousal support, alimony is money paid from one spouse to the other. In its ideal state, it would allow the recipient of the payments to continue his or her lifestyle just as it was before the divorce, but that is rarely the case. Resentments against spouses, as well as financial and employment constraints, create a wide gap between what will be paid and what would be needed to keep the status quo.

Traditionally, alimony was from husband to wife, as most couples followed the conventional pattern of the husband working and the wife staying home to raise the children and keep the house. In these cases, the wife may have lacked education or job skills, and may have been home for many years prior to the divorce, making entering the workforce nearly impossible. There are still many couples who fit this pattern, and in these cases, spousal support will be ordered.

Today, wife to husband support has become more common, as has the lack of any support at all being ordered. In our culture of two-income families, there is often no need for one spouse to support the other after a divorce because both have been working full-time throughout the marriage.

Most states have what is known as "no-fault" divorces, meaning that neither party will be listed as being at fault for the dissolution of the marriage. Fifteen states allow only no-fault divorces, and many others allow either type. In states that allow fault to be a factor in divorce, such fault may come into play during the support portion of the divorce.

Factors Affecting Spousal Support Judgments

Whether you and your spouse negotiate support or the court orders it, the following must be taken into consideration:

- The payer's ability to make payments
- The need of the recipient
- The spouses' ages and health conditions
- The standard of living during the marriage
- The duration of the marriage
- The ability of each spouse to earn an income
- The recipients' contributions to the marriage that cannot be quantified monetarily
- Whether the recipient can be self-supporting at the time of divorce or in the future
- Taxes

The list is long with good reason: There are many factors that must be weighed when requesting support or entering into an agreement of support.

Types of Alimony

When determining the length of time that spousal support will be paid, courts will take into consideration the purpose of alimony and award either *rehabilitative alimony* or *modifiable/non-modifiable alimony*.

Rehabilitative spousal support, true to its name, is ordered in cases where one spouse could eventually support himself or herself if given time and opportunity to finish a degree or obtain job skills that may have been ignored or unnecessary during the course of the marriage. This type of support will have a pre-determined time limit, mutually agreed upon by both spouses and made legal by the courts. If you are pursuing rehabilitative maintenance while raising children, you may want to give yourself a liberal timetable for completing your education or training so that you will be able to support yourself by the time the support period is over.

Here is a good example of rehabilitative support. James and Brenda have been married for ten years. They married just as James was finishing college and Brenda was a junior. She never finished school, as their first child was due to arrive in their first year of marriage, followed shortly thereafter by two more children within five years. James attended graduate school, while Brenda cared for the children, and he eventually went on to become a college professor. At the time of their divorce, Brenda had no job skills and had not finished her degree in accounting, and she would not be able to support herself without finishing her degree.

Their divorce was an amicable one, and they were able to construct a rehabilitative spousal support agreement that would allow Brenda to complete not only her undergraduate degree, but also, concurrently, her master's in accounting. At the end of the support agreement, Brenda will be qualified to work in her field and should be able to obtain a job that will give her the self-sufficiency she needs.

In contrast to rehabilitative alimony, both modifiable and non-modifiable alimony are considered permanent support programs. This variety of alimony ends with either the death of the payer of support or when the recipient of the support remarries, unless a specific time is negotiated with the courts. The distinctions between the two are important considerations as you enter this phase of the divorce process.

In the case of modifiable alimony, either party may petition the court for a reduction or increase in the payments; the payer is requesting the reduction and the recipient is requesting the increase. As life circumstances change due to health concerns, living arrangements, or employment status, either spouse may find it necessary to change the amount of support being paid. A petition is not a guarantee of a change to the support order, but the opportunity for change does exist.

Non-modifiable spousal support is just that: not modifiable — unless, of course, you and your ex-spouse want to hire lawyers and start the entire process from the beginning, where you would each have to agree to a new order of support. The advantage to non-modifiable support is that the payment is a constant. For the recipient, that means that even if life changes, with remarriage or a better-paying job, the support amount remains the same. For the payer, the constancy of payments can give you some solace in that you will not be petitioned to pay for additional expenses later on. The disadvantage to both parties is that the set amount may not work for them when life is a little different. If you are receiving spousal support and are laid off from your job due to health reasons, you cannot easily modify the support order. Similarly, if you are the payer and happen upon unfortunate financial conditions, you will still be obligated to adhere to the constraints of the original support order.

Determining Spousal Support

Not every divorce involves spousal support. If you have been employed for most of your marriage, or if your marriage lasted less than five years, spousal support will most likely not be a part of your divorce settlement.

Many states have a formula, called a financial schedule for alimony, to determine the amount of support. Your lawyer or your local legal aid office can inform you about the details of your state and county's procedures regarding support. Get this information before you begin the process of petitioning for support because this determination will be important in how much support you will receive or have to pay.

In the absence of a financial schedule for alimony, the judge will take many factors into account. If your children are younger than school age, a support order will most likely be in place to help the custodial parent manage the care for those children. At eight to ten years of marriage, an award of alimony is likely, with its goal being the maintenance of the standard of living during the marriage for the spouse who cannot otherwise manage to maintain this on his or her own. Men are increasingly becoming the recipient of spousal support, as many women are the breadwinners in their marriage, and their husbands may work outside the home or may have taken on the traditionally female role of caring for young children.

Once you and your spouse have split up the marital assets, you should have a good idea of how much alimony you will need or, if you will be the payer, how much you can afford to contribute. If you can negotiate a settlement together, the process will be much quicker and smoother, but the court system is in place to help protect both parties and establish an equitable support order.

If you are seeking rehabilitative support, you will need to have a rough estimate of how long it will take to obtain the skills you need and the approximate cost. If you are petitioning the court for a more permanent solution, be sure you have taken all variables into consideration, including both your reasonable expenses and your ex-spouse's ability to make those payments over time.

Child Support

If you are heading into a divorce with children, their well-being is likely your first priority. Unlike spousal support, child support is universally ordered in cases of divorce with dependent children because each parent is unequivocally responsible for the care of their children. Like spousal support, child support can be a volatile topic; child rearing may have been one of the more difficult issues in your marriage.

In an ideal situation, both parents would determine the actual needs of the child and come to an agreement on the amount of support necessary for them to continue their life as before the divorce. The family court system attempts to keep the status quo for children of divorce, but when a household is split in two, it is difficult to fund both of those homes, as well as continue life as normal for the children.

Custody and its Impact on Child Support

Once custody of children is established, the determination of child support, meaning who is going to pay it and how much, can begin. In cases where one parent maintains primary physical custody of children, the other parent will likely bear a large burden of financial support. It would seem obvious that the parent who has the day-to-day responsibility for the children would need financial support from the spouse who may only have custody on weekends. Even in an amicable divorce, however, there can be disputes as to how much is necessary, and arguments over how the money is spent once the child support payments begin.

In a situation where custody is shared, which is becoming more common these days, the support burden is not as clear-cut. If you have the children alternating weeks, or share custody during the week, it may not be clear which parent has the responsibility for providing support.

Your lawyer can advise you of your state's process for determining support — either the income shares method or the percentage of income model.

Income Shares Method: This model takes into consideration the entire household's income and the percentage each spouse contributed to that amount. If you are the non-custodial parent and made 80 percent of the income for your family, your payments will be that percentage of the total expenses calculated for your children.

Percentage of Income Method: Some states employ either a flat or varying percentage model to determine support based on the number and possibly ages of your children. The varying percentage is based on income level.

Check your state's Web site for information if you are in the planning stage for custody and divorce. You may be able to use a calculator there to estimate what your child support will look like.

How to Determine What You Will Need

Now that you have a better idea what spousal support and child support are and how they function, let us look at how to go about figuring what it will cost to live separate lives and take care of your children in this new family structure.

Determining Spousal Support

You will want to carefully evaluate your needs for spousal support because, unlike child support, it cannot be assumed that you will receive alimony. You will likely be required to meet certain standards, such as:

- **Length of Marriage:** Eight or more years.

- **Number and Ages of Children:** The younger your children are, the more likely you will be awarded alimony.

- **Ability to Earn an Income:** Again, this may depend on your need to care for children and/or your employability.

If you are keeping your home, that payment will be part of the equation, but you must also carefully evaluate your expenses and your current income. You cannot expect that you will be living life exactly as before your divorce; circumstances have changed. Here is a brief list of expenses to consider:

- Property taxes on your home
- Car payments, insurance, maintenance, and fuel
- Utilities
- Health insurance
- Food
- Clothing
- Debt payments

You may find that now is the time to take a long, clear look at your expenses and your needs versus your wants. The first things to go in times of financial stress are the little luxuries you may have become accustomed to. You may even realize that a near total overhaul of your lifestyle is necessary to maintain a comfortable standard of living after the divorce.

Even if you are employed, you should evaluate your ability to maintain your household once the divorce is finalized. You may find that you could benefit from rehabilitative support or temporary support for the transitional period following the divorce. Now is the time to advocate for yourself rather than cut and run. Put in the time to petition for what you and your children need, and it will pay off down the road.

Determining Child Support

Establishing child support is an intricate process, and it may depend heavily on the tone of your relationship with your soon-to-be ex-spouse. If you are in a custody battle and can barely stand to be in the same room together, you will find agreeing on child support to be one more obstacle on the journey to fully end the marriage.

If you will have primary physical custody for your children, you must factor all expenses related to their needs into a request for support. You will still be subject to your state's policy on support, but those are just to establish the minimum that must be paid; you and your spouse can come up with whatever arrangement suits the both of you. Here are some of the biggest expenses to consider:

- Education costs
- Food
- Sports or other activities the child is already enrolled in
- School activities, including field trips
- Clothing
- Medical expenses
- Miscellaneous (this is the big one when it comes to kids)
- A share of household expenses

Also a consideration will be who will carry the health insurance for your children (see sidebar on QMCSO for more information).

A change in circumstances after the divorce will allow you to petition the court for a change in the child support order. If your daughter is pursuing an Olympic soccer dream and needs thousands of dollars to reach that goal, you can ask for more support. Of course, just petitioning does not mean you will get more support, but it is reassuring to know that you will be able to request a modification of the original support order as needed in the future. It may not be simple to change your support order, but it will be important to the well-being of your child to keep the support amount in line with his or her changing needs.

Negotiating and Settling on an Agreement

If you and your spouse have been able to negotiate your own settlement, you will be in a better position financially than if you left it up to the court. You will still need to look out for certain factors, such as the length of support and the details of the agreement. In an amicable situation, you may feel some sense of complacency, but it is still vital for you to understand all the details of your agreement.

If you are heading to court, or are still negotiating with your spouse, here are some tips to remember:

Be Reasonable and Honest: If your spouse is unable to make the payments in good faith, no court order is going to change that. Be up-front about you and your children's needs, and be rational in the scope of your request.

Back it Up: Provide documentation for your requirements: mortgage information, school tuition bills, medical expenses from the prior year — anything and everything that will support your claims for support. Courts love documents.

Keep the Children Out of It: Like it or not, you are embarking on a new stage of life, and your children are watching your (and your ex's) every move. The non-custodial spouse is still their parent, and they are likely attached to him or her. Witnessing or, even worse, participating in financial wrangling will make your children blame themselves for the divorce, and may lead them to resent both of you in the future. Divorce is for adults only.

Use Legal Representation: Whenever possible and affordable, have a reputable attorney protect your interests. It is his or her job to know family law and to help guide you through the ins and outs of support. You would not go into a jungle without a guide; do not go into your divorce without one, either.

It is All About the Taxes

While child support is never tax deductible because the contributions are made from pre-tax dollars, spousal support is tax deductible for the payer, but the recipient must declare it as income and pay taxes on all payments.

The IRS is meticulous, so if you want to stay honest come tax time, here are some points to remember:

- Only payments of cash or cash equivalent may be included as tax deductions for the payer. If your ex-spouse buys you groceries, he cannot then deduct those expenses as alimony on his taxes. The same holds true for larger items, such as a vehicle or even a home.

- Keep it in writing. Only the amount of spousal support ordered by the court may be deducted from the payer's taxes as alimony. Any money given or received outside the written agreement will not be considered payment of support by the IRS.

- You must be maintaining separate households and filing separate tax returns.

- Alimony and child support are not the same thing. When it comes to your taxes, the two cannot mix.

Qualified Medical Child Support Order (QMCSO)

In a world of terminology and abbreviations, this one may be one of the most important to know and understand. This order, a result of federal law enacted to protect children from loss of health care coverage, requires that a child be covered under the health insurance policy of the non-custodial parent.

What that means for you is that if your children will be living with you, but you do not have health insurance coverage, your ex-spouse will be required to keep them on his or her employer's policy. Many times, a parent is forced into the workplace by divorce and may have to take either a low-paying or entry-level job, which may not offer health insurance coverage. This is where the QMCSO comes into play. This order will be a legal document; part of the order of support.

Child Support and Taxes

- Child support payments are not tax deductible for the payer, and are not reportable as income for the recipient. Essentially, the IRS views child support payments the same as money spent on the children as though the family were still intact.

- Only one parent may claim a child as a dependent in any given year.

- In the case of shared custody, parents may each claim different children or claim all children in alternating years.

- Only the parent who retains physical custody of the children may claim the child care credit, and he or she may only claim the amount he or she contributes to such expenses.

What If My Spouse Will not Pay Support?

You hear enough about "deadbeat" parents for it to be worrisome for anyone facing divorce. Your state should have guidelines in place to deal with non-payment of court-ordered child support; some of these include:

- **Court Hearings:** The non-paying parent can be subject to jail time if the child support is not paid.

- **Wage Garnishment:** The court can rule that child support payments be taken directly out of the non-custodial parent's paycheck at a percentage rate to bring payments up-to-date.

- **Property Liens:** You can be entitled to a chunk of your ex-spouse's real estate if he or she does not pay up.

- **Report to Credit Bureaus:** Having an effect on your ex's credit may be a good way to encourage him or her to stay current with support payments.

All attempts to settle child support claims should be taken through the court system. Keep in mind that your child support order is a legal document with real consequences for the payer. Any action taken outside the court system cannot be reinforced legally.

Tax Terms to Know

1040 Form – The standard IRS form used by individuals to file their income tax return.

Adjusted Gross Income (AGI) – A person's taxable income.

Child Tax Credit – A credit given on a taxpayer's return for each minor child they are claiming.

Deduction – All allowable expenses that can be used to reduce your taxable income.

Dependent – A child, spouse, or parent who relies on you financially.

Earned Income – Income from wages, salary, tips, commissions, and bonuses.

Earned Income Credit – A refundable tax credit offered by the government.

Estate Tax – The taxes charged to the estate of someone who has died.

Exemption – A deduction offered to help lower your taxable income level.

Filing Status – The way in which you file your taxes; as a married couple, single individual, or otherwise.

Itemized Deduction – Deductions from taxable adjusted gross income for money spent on specific goods and services throughout the year.

Passive Income – Earnings from any business in which you are not an active participant.

Property Tax – Taxes owed on a property.

Tax Credit – A dollar-for-dollar reduction on your taxes.

Taxable Income – The amount the government can tax.

Tax Tips for Non-Custodial Parents:

The custodial parent gains most of the tax benefits for the child, unless other arrangements are made within the couple's divorce settlement. Things get a little harder when parents share custody in a joint custody agreement. Because only one parent can usually take the tax benefits offered for children, you will have to decide which ones go to which parent during your divorce settlement. Here are a few of the main ones to consider when hammering out these important issues during the divorce:

The Dependent Exemption

Always given to the custodial parent, this exemption can reduce the receiver's and cannot be shared by parents.

Income Adjustment

There are two ways to deduct secondary education costs as a parent. You can claim an adjustment to your gross income for up to $3,000, or you can take the flat education credit, but not both.

Itemized Deductions

It doesn't matter with whom a child resides, either (or both) can claim the deductions for medical costs they paid out during the year for the child as long as the total amount does not exceed 7.5 percent of their income.

Child Care Credit

It is important to understand that only a custodial parent can claim the child care credit on their income tax return, even if the non-custodial parent claims the child as a dependent on their own return.

Child Tax Credit

The maximum child tax credit is $600 per qualifying child.

Education Credit

Only the parent claiming the child as a dependent has the legal right to claim the education credit offered by the IRS.

Earned Income Credit

Worth as much as $4,140, the EIC is only available to the parent with physical custody.

PART III

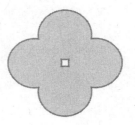

Moving On

CHAPTER 12

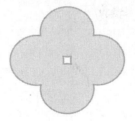

Dealing with Your Grief

Whether you are dealing with the death of a spouse or the death of a marriage, you will need to find ways to deal with your grief to cope with the changes that lie ahead.

Losing a spouse is always difficult. Even when a death is imminent or a divorce expected, you will still need to undergo the emotional roller coaster ride of grief. One way to handle the ups and downs you will likely experience is to first understand what grief is so you will know what to expect.

The Role of Grief in Our Lives

Grief is a strong, overwhelming sense of sadness that can make you feel numb to or removed from your daily lives. Not just a matter of feeling badly, grief offers a way to deal with emotions and move through the losses in your lives.

While it is impossible to control how long it will take for you as an individual to work through your own grief, there are a few natural stages to watch out for. As you find yourself experiencing each one, you can feel the relief of knowing that you are moving beyond your initial sadness toward a healthy return to normal living. The five main stages of grief are:

1. **Denial and Isolation.**
   Initially after experiencing a loss, people tend to deny that anything has really changed and try to go on as before. However, as denial deepens, individuals tend to retreat into their own inner sanctuary, withdrawing from outside contact and social interactions. Lasting from a few weeks to a few months, this is a common response to losing a spouse, or in some cases, even a marriage.

2. **Anger.**
   Anger is the second phase of the grieving process, leaving those left behind furious at their spouse for causing them so much pain — even if they are dead. Other forms of anger may be thrust toward the world around them or other people in their lives for letting this bad thing happen, or even themselves for not finding a way to stop the death of their spouse or their divorce.

3. **Bargaining.**
   Once the grieving person realizes that this painful change is here to stay, he or she may begin bargaining with God to make it better, or even an ex to come back, thinking that bargaining will make all of the pain disappear.

4. **Depression.**
   Not always an instantaneous reaction to grief, depression comes near the end of the grieving process, although this stage may last the longest for some. Once the reality of his or her loss hits home, the survivor often feels numb, although anger and sadness may remain as underlining conflict continues.

5. **Acceptance.**
   The last, and final, stage of the grieving process comes when the anger, sadness, and mourning have tapered off and the marriage survivor finally accepts the reality of his or her loss.

People grieve in different ways and at a different pace. One new widow may find a sense of release after his or her spouse's long, drawn-out illness and be able to move forward somewhat quickly. Another widow may find himself or herself stuck in one stage or another for a long period of time, unable to move forward toward final acceptance.

The same holds true for those going through a divorce. No matter how expected a divorce is, those left cleaning up the pieces of a broken marriage may find it difficult to move forward. While the outside world may tell the grieving widow or the grieving divorcées to "get on with life," it is important for those undergoing these devastating changes to accept their own unique style and pace of grieving to ensure that they do not rush through one or more of its stages, only to find themselves backsliding in the future. Eventually every stage must be experienced and the feelings dealt with, or the sufferer will not be able to find acceptance and fulfillment in his or her own life in the future.

People have their own set of unique experiences, coping mechanisms, and attitudes, which may influence their reaction to grief. This can influence the way they grieve and help determine how long it will take for us to move from stage to stage successfully.

Past Experience

The things individuals have experienced in the past have a tremendous impact on the way they handle adversity in the present — especially loss. These depend on the other types of loss you have experienced in your lives and how traumatic these losses were. You will draw on them to let you know how your present experiences will be. If for instance, a child experiences the death of a parent at a young age and is left to deal with his or her fear alone with little or no support, he or she may react to the current loss in one of two ways:

1. By seeking help and support from those around him or her.

2. Or by retreating within himself or herself, believing they must take care of themselves.

In addition, if this same child was left to believe that he or she could not openly express his or her grief as a child, he or she will often find it difficult to show much emotion at his or her current loss. This can be devastating as the child tries to move from grief stage to grief stage because an important part of dealing is acknowledging emotions and accepting them as normal.

Another important aspect to consider when determining your grief style is to look at your own mental state. If you are prone to depression or nervous tendencies, than you may find dealing with any substantial loss more difficult and consider seeking trained medical or mental health help to get you through this time.

Never underestimate how past events in your life may be affecting your ability to deal with the loss of your spouse — whether through death or divorce — right now. Look for clues to help you better see why you may be feeling a certain way, or why you may find yourself stuck in one grief stage longer than others.

Your Relationship with Your Spouse

The relationship that you had with your spouse can also influence the intensity and the duration of your grief. It is not just the person, but also the role he or she played in your life that you have lost. Even if you were not emotionally close, but you depended on him or her a great deal for making the decisions in your life, you may find it difficult to stand on your own two feet now that he or she is gone.

In addition, if your spouse was your main emotional support and best friend, then you will not only grieve the loss of your spouse and marriage, but the loss of your confidante as well. This situation can make it even more difficult to deal with your loss, and can extend the life of your individual grieving process.

Everyone's relationships are different, however. Some people miss the actual person, while others miss the perception or the stability that this important relationship brought to their lives. When this tie is broken, they may feel lost, abandoned, or both. This must all be considered when dealing with your grief to help you better understand your reactions to it.

Circumstances Surrounding Your Loss

Also affecting how you will grieve are the circumstances surrounding your spouse's death or the disintegration of your marriage. Did your spouse die suddenly, or were you his or her sole caregiver for the duration of a long illness? Did your marriage begin to crumble under the stress of an affair, or over a long period of neglect? The circumstances surrounding your loss are important in determining how you are going to come to an acceptance of the loss.

Those individuals who help their spouse through a long-term illness may have already experienced many of the stages of grief, and when the death finally occurs, they are able to move quickly toward a restoration in their life, much to the surprise (and sometimes even dismay) of those around them. Does this mean that they loved their spouse less than the person who locks himself or herself away for months, retreating into his or her own life of grief? Certainly not. Each finds a way to grieve in his or her own way, with some beginning the process earlier than others.

In contrast, a spouse who finds himself or herself suddenly widowed may find it difficult to move beyond his or her grief because of the suddenness of the event. Without warning, his or her entire life changes, leaving him or her feeling lost. This situation can cause severe anxiety and depression in some and must be considered when trying to get through the grieving process. Guilt too may be a factor, as those left behind may find themselves reliving their last moments with their loved ones and wishing they could have handled those moments better.

Present Influences

Influences in your past are as important as influences in the here and now that can affect your grieving process. For instance, younger people may find it easier to bounce back than those who have been with a spouse for decades. But middle-aged individuals may be best prepared because they have the maturity and understanding to accept their loss and know how to rebuild their life, while those who are younger may not, and those who are older and more frail may not be as resilient.

Secondary losses are also a factor. If a death or divorce causes major financial stress, the loss of a home or even a custody battle, the grieving process may be exacerbated.

Personality too should be considered, as some people are more apt to fight back, while others may tend to sit back and let things happen to them. A person's ability to become self-sufficient can help push him or her from one grief stage to the next.

Lastly, consider a person's social, cultural, and ethnic background when determining his or her grief style. If people have a supportive network or ritual that brings comfort and strength, they are more apt to move forward more quickly.

The most important thing to remember when dealing with your grief is to understand that every phase is normal and that you must experience each stage in its entirety before moving on to the next. No one can push you forward faster than you are ready to go. By understanding the uniqueness of your grief, you can find the support you will need to recognize when you need to be alone to work through your feelings, and when you should reach out to those around you for help.

The Benefits of Finding a Support Group

When you are feeling alone and feeling like no one else understands what you are going through, joining a support and bereavement group can help you make an emotional connection with others who can truly say they understand.

According to the Mayo Clinic, a bereavement group can "provide and share information ranging from disease research and new medications to how a bereaved person can cope during the first year after a loved one's death." People involved say this exchange of information is one of the most valuable elements of participating in a support or bereavement group.

More than that, a good support group can give you a safe place to release any powerful emotions that you may be holding back.

Before joining any support group, consider what type might suit your age, experience, and personality best. Some people like small, intimate groups best because they offer a feeling of security, while others may prefer a larger group where they can remain somewhat anonymous.

Also consider whether you would prefer to have a health care professional or a layperson leading the group. While both offer benefits, the structure can change the way the group is held and the focus it has.

Support Groups to Try

Here are a few national support groups for people handling loss recommended by The Mayo Clinic:

- **The Compassionate Friends**
  P.O. Box 3696
  Oak Brook, IL 60522-3696
  Telephone — (877) 969-0010

- **Grief Watch**
  2116 NE 18th Avenue
  Portland, OR 97212
  Telephone — (503) 284-7426

- **GriefShare**
  E-mail address — **info@griefshare.org**

When looking for a support group in your area, be sure to check with the grief counselors at your local hospital, hospice, or other agency. They can often steer you to just the right group to meet your family's needs.

Signs of Depression

Depression is often associated with grief. After all, losing a spouse is a devastating event that can leave you feeling lost and alone. While some degree of temporary depression is considered normal during this difficult time in your life, be sure to watch for these signs of a more serious bout with depression, which may indicate a need for professional help and/or medication to get you through:

- A loss of interest

- Sadness

- Hopelessness

- Unreasonable crying

- Sleep disorders

- Problems concentrating

- Weight changes (either gaining or losing weight for no apparent reasons)

- Irritability

- Restlessness

- Feelings of worthlessness

- No interest in sex

- Suicidal behaviors and/or thoughts

- Unexplained physical complaints and problems

When to Seek Medical Advice

Feeling sad is completely normal right now, especially with all the changes you are undergoing, but if you find these feelings lingering, it may be time to admit that you need help.

The first place to turn is your medical doctor. Do not be surprised if he/she refers you to a mental health provider. This certainly does not mean that you are crazy; rather, these professionals are able to give you the tools you will need to move past your grief and on with your life, despite your recent loss.

When You Have Suicidal Thoughts

Left unchecked, your depression may increase, leaving you in danger of hurting yourself as a way to qualm your anxiety and sadness. If you find yourself thinking about suicide, call 911 immediately, or:

- Call someone you love

- Contact your doctor or a mental health professional

- Call your spiritual leader

- Head to the local Emergency Room

- Call a crisis center or hot line

Feeling depressed after a loss is normal, to a degree. The important thing is to recognize when these feelings have reached a danger point for yourself in any manner – either physically or emotionally. There is plenty of help out there for you, if you reach for it.

CHAPTER 13

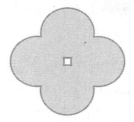

Dealing with Life's Practicalities

U nfortunately, while you find yourself dealing with the mental roller coaster of your new life, its financial impact, and the emotional upheaval it has caused you and your family, life's practicalities must be dealt with.

First things first: It is time to redo your will. Chances are that your will lists your spouse as the beneficiary to all of your assets. Now that your spouse is no longer in the picture, it is important to make changes to your will, power of attorney, and life insurance policies. This is especially important in the case of a divorce, where you may not want to give your ex the power for life-and-death decisions (or your money), should you be permanently disabled or even die. Until you make the necessary changes on all of your legal documents, your living spouse would remain the decision maker in these situations.

Of course, in the event that your spouse has died, you would be leaving everything up to your children and their new guardians — assuming that you indeed named guardians in your current will.

Why Estate Planning Is So Important

There are a lot of reasons for planning your estate now, but here are a few of the most important reasons why you should take the time to deal with these important matters:

- A solid estate plan will enable you to take care of the people and organizations you care for after your death. Without a legal record of how you want your assets spent, they may go to people and things you would rather not support.

- It arranges for the care of your minor children (or those requiring long-term care) in a manner in which you control. Without a will, the courts would decide who your children reside with or which long-term facility would be best for their care.

- It legally transfers all of your property to the beneficiaries of your choice.

- Helps you control (even after your death) how financial disbursements are made. For instance, you can designate periodic disbursements to minors on their 18th, 21st, 25th, and even 30th birthdays if you so choose.

- It helps to eliminate many inheritance taxes owed by your beneficiaries.

- Helps to speed the entire process for your beneficiaries.

- Helps you to plan for the future of any business you may own and/ or run, should you be incapacitated or even die.

- Can set a funeral plan in place, allowing you to make these decisions so your family does not have to in the event of your death.

Now that you understand the importance of dealing with these changes right away, take a look at the documents that need to be changed:

Your Power Of Attorney

In the event that you are permanently or temporarily unable to make decisions for yourself or any children you may be responsible for due to an illness or severe injury, a legal durable powers of attorney will allow a third party to step in. This third party can take care of everything from paying your bills, to making decisions regarding the care of your home and children. Of course, you will want to take care when choosing a power of attorney because the person you appoint will have total and complete access to your finances and will have all legal rights to do what they want with them.

In addition, you may want to consider appointing a Durable Power of Attorney for Health Care (DPCH), which will enable you to delegate someone else to make medical decisions for you during an emergency or your incapacity. Because of the many laws regarding such decisions, be sure to have your DPCH drafted by a lawyer in accordance to local and state laws where you live.

Your Living Will

In some states, a living will may be required in addition to a DPCH for someone else to make necessary decisions regarding the extension of your life using extraordinary means, or the dissolution of them. A living will carefully outlines your wishes in regard to life support, organ donations, and autopsies. This may be the only way you have of making your own decisions in a life or death situation.

Your Last Will and Testament

Most couples name each other as their main beneficiary, with their children listed as secondary ones in their last will and testament. This action gives the surviving spouse the rights to all estate matters and decisions after your death. But what happens when your spouse is gone? Your will is an important document meant to tell the courts who should receive your assets and take care of any minor children left behind.

Be sure to carefully outline how all assets should be divided and who should retain guardianship of your children. Many parents also take the added step of appointing an executor to handle all monies held in trust for the children separate from the guardians to ensure that any inheritances are not squandered by the adults caring for the children before they can have access to it themselves.

You are not required to appoint your ex-spouse as your children's legal guardian after your death if you retain sole custody. However, many parents do, especially if the spouse in question has remained involved in the children's life and care giving after the divorce.

Establishing a Trust

While your will is designed to specify who gets what after your death, a trust can tie certain monies to specific purposes such as college costs, wedding costs for your children, and more. Implementing a trust allows you to keep a certain amount of control over your assets, even after your death.

For most people, a trust is only established as a way to handle child care costs for guardians while maintaining a certain amount of inheritance for the children. However, if your assets equal more than $600,000, a trust can be a useful way to save inheritance fees and taxes, and to ensure that your children will not squander their inheritance on things you would disapprove of.

As is the case with most legal and financial documents, there are several types of trusts to consider:

- **Testamentary Trusts:** These are created by will at the death of the grantor and cannot be modified except by certain provisions in the will.

- **Inter Vivos Trusts:** This is a type of trust that takes effect while the grantor is still alive and includes both revocable and irrevocable trusts.

- **Revocable Living Trust:** These can be changed or revoked any time during the grantor's lifetime. They are mainly used to avoid probate, and for ease and flexibility. They offer no estate tax consequences and are often used by adults with no relatives.

- **Irrevocable Trusts:** This is a permanent trust that cannot be changed unless it follows strict perimeters outlined in the original trust. These trusts are used by the super-wealthy to avoid estate and inheritance taxes.

- **Marital Deduction Trusts:** This is a trust that allows you to transfer up to $600,000 in assets to a new spouse without tax penalty.

Preparing an estate plan is especially important for single parents, who will likely want to ensure that their children retain ownership of their property and assets after their death. Without a will or trust in place, the courts will have the last say in regard to your money and your children, which may not be what you would want. Another aspect to consider: Should you remarry, your new spouse could be awarded more than half of your total estate following your death, leaving your children out in the cold, unless your wishes are clearly and legally documented. While you may not want to consider your untimely demise, especially at a time like this, it is important to take the appropriate measures to protect your children and your assets should the worst happen in the future.

What to Consider When Drafting Your Will

You may have always thought of your will as a simple list of who gets what. It may be that, but it is also much more. A last will and testament is a way for you to outline your wishes regarding where your money will go after your death; who will retain ownership of your property, assets, and personal belongings; who will care for your children; how your children will be cared for; who will care for your pets; how much your favorite charities will get; if your organs will be donated; and even how you would like your funeral to take place. It can be as simple or as detailed as you would like.

Where to Begin

There are many ways to write a basic will. You can purchase a fill-in-the-blank one, use a computer program to write your own, or have an attorney draft one for you. It all depends on how complicated your life is, how many people will be featured as your beneficiaries and, of course, how much money you have.

What to Include in Your Will

Once you have decided how to write your will, you will need to know what to include. Here is a list to get you started:

- Your name.
- The date
- The tile "Will"
- A statement revoking all previous wills.
- The name of those who you would like to handle the financial aspect of your will
- The names of the chosen guardians for your children.
- Any specific bequests you may have.

Where to Keep Your Will

True, you don't want just anyone to have access to this important document, but you really do need to let the people who will make sure your wishes are followed know where your will is. Make sure your executor and attorney have a copy, and keep a spare in a safe-deposit box.

It is important that your executor know where your original will is. Without it the copy can be revoked by the courts and your assets disbursed by a judge.

Where to Keep Your Important Documents

No matter how organized or unorganized you are, the fact remains: If your survivors do not know where to locate your important documents, then all of your pre-planning is in waste.

Here are a few places to consider storing your most vital documents:

- **Your Will:** You should have only one original will, but keep copies in at least three places, including your attorney's office, your safety deposit box, and with a close relative. Your executor should hold the original. Or at least keep it in a safe place within your home that can be easily located.

- **Your Living Trust:** Keep this in the same location as your will. Any deeds belonging to the trust should also be kept there.

- **Your Living Will:** The best place to keep copies of your living will are with your primary care physician, or any specialist handling life-threatening diseases, your local hospital, and a close friend or relative who will likely be called in an emergency situation.

- **Your Durable Power of Attorney:** Keep the original on-file with your attorney and give copies to those listed as the executor of the document.

- **Burial Instructions:** Because they will be needed immediately, keep any burial instructions where they can be easily found and tell someone close to you where they are. Some good choices here include your pastor, doctor, a close friend, and next of kin.

Why You Should Hire a Lawyer to Write Your Will

When it comes to drafting a will, it is a good idea to have a professional do it. No matter how big or small your final estate, failing to hire a lawyer to write it for you could cost your survivors in extra taxes, plus cause delays and heartaches they do not need.

Here are several good reasons why you should consider hiring a lawyer to write this important document:

- It will get done. Left on your own, you may tend to procrastinate when doing something as morbid as writing your own will — even when you realize how important it truly is.

- Simple wills are fairly cheap. Most cost between $300-$1,000, unless, of course, your estate is rather large and contains a lot of special attention.

- It will be hard to contest. A will drafted by an attorney stands up in court, while those written on your own may be subject to scrutiny and eventually voided by a judge.

- An attorney can give you solid advice regarding taxes and fees that may be required by your beneficiaries unless action steps are taken to avoid them.

- An attorney can explain the entire probate process in detail and help you prepare for it within your will.

CHAPTER 14

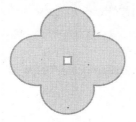

Securing Your Child's Future

With college costs rising every year, it may seem like an impossible task to save enough to get your children to college, especially considering the new financial burdens you are responsible for.

Depending on your children's ages, you may have more time to save. There are several good options for saving for your child's college education; take a look at each to help you choose what is best for you.

Educational Savings Accounts

Formerly known as an Education IRA, the Educational Savings Account (ESA) is a tax-free savings plan that must be used for educational expenses by the time the recipient is 30 years old. Here are some of the program's highlights:

- They are custodial accounts

- They may also be used for "qualified expenses," in addition to tuition, fees, and room and board associated with college expenses, such as computers and books. After 2010, K-12 expenses will no longer qualify.

- Annual contributions are limited to $2,000. After 2010, annual contributions will be lowered to $500.

- Income limits for the holder of the account are $110,000 per individual and $220,000 per couple if the account is held jointly.

- Visit **www.savingforcollege.com/intro_to_esas** for more information.

The 529 Plan

The 529 plan is an investment plan that has grown in popularity in recent years, as it allows money to be put into an educational account, free from federal taxes. Interest also grows tax-free. There are three basic types of 529 plans: the independent, the state prepaid plan, and the regular 529 plan. While they do vary from state to state, most have the following features in common:

- Contributions to a 529 plan are not taxable when withdrawn for educational expenses

- There are no maximum contributions

- Funds may only be used for necessary costs associated with college, such as tuition, room and board, and fees

- There are no income restrictions regarding contributors; anyone may open a 529 account for a child

The state prepaid 529, also known as a Prepaid Education Arrangement (PEA), is a good way to save for a child's college education now, as it allows you to pre-pay for college credits at today's rate, and use them any time in the future.

Education Savings Bonds

While there is not a specific educational bond, all Series I bonds and those Series EE bonds purchased after 1989 can be used to fund educational expenses without a tax impact.

- Bonds in your child's name will not be subject to the tax-free use for school

- Bonds have a fixed rate of return that cannot compete with 529 or ESA plans with the same amount invested

- Bonds may be used to fund tuition and required fees

UGMA/UTM

Both considered custodial accounts, the Uniform Gifts to Minors Act (UGMA) and the Uniform Transfer to Minor Act (UTM) are ways to give money to a minor child without using the format of a legal trust. An important fact to remember with both of these products is that the money does belong to your child and does not have to be used for education.

Whatever your financial situation, it is important to start saving for college now using one or more of these plans. Being prepared for whatever lies ahead is an important way to ensure that your child gets the college education he or she deserves.

Create an Action Plan for your Family:

When it comes to savings for your child's college education, it is never too early (or too late) to begin. The best way to ensure that you will have the money when you need it is to create an action plan now, while you are evaluating all of your spending habits and re-evaluating your lifestyle.

Here are a few tips to get you started:

1. Get your current finances under control. Make a budget that includes retirement savings and college savings, even if these are modest at first.
2. Make a rough budget for college. If college is still more than a decade away, just estimate what you think you will need — then triple it — and start tackling one bite at a time.
3. Get your child involved. Is he or she old enough to make his or her own money? Let the child contribute, too.
4. Select a college savings plan and stick to it.

What About Children Getting Ready for College Now?

Maybe saving for your child's education is not the problem; simply getting your teen to school is. At a time when you have so much to deal with, you may not have the mindset (or patience) to deal with preparing your high school child for college and finding the money to pay for it. Get ready for this important decision by learning about the different ways you can pay for your child's education:

Financial Aid

Not sure how you are going to pay the high costs of college in addition to your other expenses? You may not need to worry. There are plenty of financial aid opportunities for students these days, including loans, grants scholarships, and service or work-study programs. Take each category individually and see how they can help you.

Student Loans

Student loans are a way to make up the difference between what free money your child receives and what you as a family are able to pay. Here are the basic loans available:

Need-Based Loans

The main attributes of need-based student loans are:

- **Low Interest Rates:** The current student loan rate (for all loans disbursed after July 1, 2006) is a fixed 6.8 percent.

- **Deferment of Payment:** Your child will not be responsible for re-payment of the loan until his or her education is either completed or terminated. Student loans are also simple to defer in the case of un-employment or economic hardship once education is completed.

- **In-School Government Subsidy of Interest:** While your child is attending college, the government pays the accruing interest on the student loan. This subsidy actually continues until six months after graduation, essentially providing a "grace period" during which no interest will be added to the balance of the loan. This would be similar to driving your car for four years and then starting to make the payments.

The Perkins Loan, the Stafford Subsidized Loan, and the Direct Loan are the three need-based, government-insured, and subsidized student loans. The basis of need does not just include how much money you can spend on your child's education, but the ratio between your income and the cost of the school that your child hopes to attend.

Of course, loans will need to be repaid, and the person doing the repaying will be your child.

Non-Need Based Loans

Unsubsidized Stafford Loans, PLUS loans, and private loans are all loans that you or your child can take to help pay for college with one major difference: interest will accrue from the day the loan money is accepted and in some cases repayment may begin while your student is still in school.

Unsubsidized Stafford Loans are not based on need and are available to most students.

PLUS (Parent Loan for Undergraduate Studies) is, as the name implies, a loan taken out by the parent. The student is not named on the loan and bears no responsibility to repayment of the loan. The interest rate on a PLUS loan is currently 8.5 percent for all loans with funds disbursed after July 1, 2006. These loans are based on credit worthiness rather than need and may be taken out for the entire amount of college costs, including books, room and board, tuition, fees, and other costs, minus, of course, any federal aid already received.

Private loans may also be available, either to students or to parents. These will vary widely, dependent on credit rating and the terms of each loan. Your child's school may be able to direct you if you are in need of a private student loan.

Grants and Scholarships

Unlike loans, grants and scholarships do not need to be repaid. Their sources can be the government, the college or university your child will attend, or a local civic organization or church community.

The Pell Grant

The federal government, following the amended legislation of the 1965 Higher Education Act, established the Pell Grant, originally named the Basic Educational Opportunity Grant (BEOG). This was designed to serve as the basis for financial aid and help to create an even playing field for students applying for aid. This is a grant-based on both need and the cost of the chosen school, taking into consideration the expense of room and board and books. Only available to students pursuing an undergraduate degree, the Pell Grant is portioned according to full- or part-time student status. The maximum yearly allocation of Pell Grant per student was $4,310 in 2007-2008. The grant is available each year of college. A chart with all possible amounts can be found at **www.ifap.ed.gov/dpcletters/attachments/2007paysch.pdf**.

Scholarships

There are hundreds of different types of scholarships available by colleges and organizations throughout the nation. Both large and small, scholarships are offered to students for a specific purpose because of their course of study, grades, or some special ability or talent.

Work-Study

Unlike working your way through college, the work-study program is part of your child's financial aid package. The federal government provides students with part-time jobs either on campus or in the surrounding community. Work-study is a way for your child to participate in paying for college and perhaps get his or her first work experience, as many of today's students do not hold jobs while in high school without the money they earn affecting their ability for other financial aid.

Everything You Need To Know About FAFSA

Before your child can even apply for any financial aid, he or she first must apply to FAFSA, otherwise known as The Free Application for Federal Student Aid. Used to help determine which programs your student qualifies for, it is the first step into getting your child the money they need for college.

Filing FAFSA Forms

According to the federal government's own federal financial aid Web site (**www.FAFSA.ed.gov**), you may choose any of these three methods to file a FAFSA.

- Apply online at **www.FAFSA.ed.gov**. This is the recommended method of filing FASFA forms.

- Request a paper FAFSA by calling the Federal Student Aid Information Center at 1-800-4-FED-AID (1-800-433-3243) or 1-319-337-5665.

Documents for Filing FAFSA

- Both you and your child's Social Security numbers
- Both you and your child's driver's license numbers
- Your most recent W-2 Forms
- The current year's federal income tax return
- The current year's untaxed income records, including Social Security benefits, veteran's benefits, welfare, or emergency living benefits
- Current bank statements

Steps for Filing FAFSA Forms

1. Gather all necessary documents, including your child's school code, which can be found on their Web site or from FAFSA itself.

1. Be aware of deadlines for FAFSA, your state, and your school as they each may be different, yet still affect the others. Application deadlines can be found on **www.fafsa.ed.gov/before003a.htm**.

1. A Personal Identification Number (PIN) is necessary to sign the FAFSA electronically for both the parent and the student. Applying is easy: Just follow the link **www.pin.ed.gov/PINWebApp/appinstr.jsp**. Once you apply for the pin, you can choose whether to view it

immediately or have it sent to you via e-mail. You may use it to file the FAFSA but nothing else until it is verified with the Social Security Administration. This process takes about one to three days. Parents and students both must have a pin. Parents can use the same pin when signing FAFSA forms for multiple siblings. Once your pin is verified it is yours permanently and will be used from year to year.

1. If you are not filing electronically, you must print and sign the signature page after you have submitted the FAFSA.

1. Before sending off your signed forms, make sure to make a copy for your own records.

TIP:

If you are feeling lost and cannot figure out how to attack all of those FAFSA forms, call the Federal Student Aid Information Center for help at 1-800-FEDAID (1-800-443-3243). TTY service is available for the hearing impaired at 1-800-730-8913. You can also e-mail your customer service questions to FederalStudentAidCustomerService@ed.gov or go for a live chat help at **www.fafsa.ed.gov/faq012.htm#faq012_1.**

What Happens Once Your Forms are Submitted?

Once you have submitted the forms, you need to be patient. It takes about a month to get your FAFSA forms back, along with an estimate of how much the government assumes that your family can pay for the college education. Of course, you can verify the status of your FAFSA by following this link: **www.fafsa.ed.gov/FOTWWebApp/follow003.jsp**.

Once the FAFSA is accepted, you will receive the Student Aid Report (SAR), followed by a letter from your child's college of choice awarding him or her a specific financial aid package.

SARS

This will also be made available to schools you have listed on your student aid report.

The SAR shows your Estimated Family Contribution (EFC), which will determine how much money your student can expect to get in grants, scholarships, in-house financial support from his or her college, and student loan eligibility.

Pell Grant eligibility will be noted in the acknowledgement letter.

How to Appeal an Award Letter

The federal government does not have a system to appeal the EFC or eligibility. You may want to contact your school's financial aid office for reconsideration if anything changes. For instance, if your spouse dies after you have already filed your child's FAFSA, by all means, contact the school officials and let them know how your situation has changed. Many are more than willing to reopen the student's financial aid account and see if more help can be offered.

In review, there are seven steps when filling out and filing the FAFSA. Hint: Organization is key:

1. Information regarding the student. Item such as Social Security number, citizenship, marital status, and grade level are needed.

2. Financial information regarding the student.

3. Student dependency status.

4. Parental financial information. For example, Social Security numbers, residency, filing status of IRS income tax return, adjusted gross income, and assets (only for dependent students).

5. Size of household (independent students only).

6. Names and codes of schools you want SAR information shared with.

7. Signature(s) on the FAFSA. Both parents and student signatures (if the student is a dependent) are required.

DID YOU KNOW?

Two of the best sources to go to for free help in filing out your FAFSA forms are the Department of Education's own Web site at **www.studentaid.ed.gov** and The Federal Student Aid Information Center at 1-800-4-FED-AID.

Ten Things You Must Know About FAFSA

You have learned about FAFSA in this chapter, but here are ten things you must know (and remember) to reap the most benefits from filing a FAFSA form:

1. **Understanding How They Count Your Family's Income**
   What your family makes during the student's junior year of high school is important, as this income will be your student's base income used by FAFSA to determine initial student aid eligibility.

2. **"As of Today" Calculations**
   While most financial calculations on the FAFSA form are based on the previous year's income, the "as of today" section requires you to report your current income, savings, and assets "as of the day you fill and sign the form."

3. **The Students' Assets**
   Students' assets are calculated differently than parents' assets. Parents are calculated at 6 percent, while students are calculated at a whopping 35 percent, which may significantly alter your final EFC (not

in your favor). For this reason, most students should refrain from keeping large amounts of savings and assets in their name.

4. **The Parents' Assets**

   While parents' assets may not cost you as much in regard to the percentage the FAFSA form calculates them at, keep in mind that most parents have a much larger amount of savings, investments, retirement, property, and business assets than their children, which could lower the amount of financial aid the student qualifies for.

5. **The Number of Students Enrolled**

   The more people in a family enrolled in college, the more financial aid each will qualify for.

6. **The Worksheets**

   Filling out all FAFSA worksheets carefully and error-free will have a positive impact on the amount of financial aid received.

7. **Family Tax Returns**

   All of the information needed for your FAFSA form will come from your family's tax return, so be sure to file early to meet all FAFSA deadlines.

8. **Verification**

   Sometimes, your school's federal aid office will require you to submit both the student's and the parents income tax returns as verification of FAFSA information.

9. **Zero EFC**

   Those who have made less than $15,000 or were not even required to file a 1040 IRS form in the previous year qualify for an immediate zero EFC, which entitles the student to the maximum amount of financial aid offered by law.

10. The SAR Report

Once FAFSA determines your EFC, they will notify you via a SAR about a month after you submit all the necessary FAFSA forms. Of course, the report can also be obtained online.

Education/Financial Aid Terms to Know...

Once you begin looking at colleges and applying for financial aid for your child, there will be find a lot of terms that you are not familiar with. Here are just a few you will need to know:

Academic Year – The length of the school year, typically from September until May.

AGI – Adjusted Gross Income.

Anticipated Graduation Date – The date the student expects to graduate.

Award Notification – An award letter from a school, which clearly outlines all financial aid offered.

Base Year – The tax year prior to the reporting year.

Bursar's Office – The college's office of finance.

Campus-Based Aid – All financial aid given to a student by the school itself.

Cost of Attendance – The "real" cost of going to college. This will include your tuition, book, room and board, etc.

Default – The failure to repay a loan.

Deferment – A suspension of payments for specific amounts of time as agreed upon by both the borrower and the lender.

Delinquent – A failure to make your loan payments as scheduled.

Dependent Student – A student who still relies on his or her parents or guardians financially.

Disburse – The release of financial aid to a student's school account.

Disclosure Statement – A statement, which lists all costs associated with a loan.

ED – The U.S. Department of Education.

EFC – Expected Family Contribution.

Enrollment Fee – A fee charged by your school to enroll as a student.

Enrollment Status – Your classification determined by how many hours you attend classes:
- *Full-time* = 12 credit hours or more
- *Three-quarter time* = nine to 11 credit hours
- *Half-time/Part-time* = six to eight credit hours
- *Less than half-time* = one to five credit hours

FAFSA – Free Application for Federal Student Aid Application.

Fellowship – A form of aid given to a student to attend graduate school to further his or her education.

FFELP – Federal Family Education Loan Program.

Financial Aid – Monies a student receives to pay for college in the form of grants, scholarships, and loans.

GPA – A student's grade point average.

Grace Period – The time until your first loan payment is due following graduation.

Independent Student – A completely financially independent student.

Lender – A financial institution that loans money.

Need – The amount you need between what your true costs will be and what your family can contribute.

Net Income – Your "bring-home" pay.

Package – The amount of money offered by the school to help your tuition.

Postsecondary – A term used to describe school after high school.

PLUS – Parent Loans for Undergraduate Students. You can learn more about this at their Web site **www.mcc.edu/6_finaid/fa_plus-loan. shtml.**

Prepaid Tuition Plan – A state-run program that sells parents' college credits at today's cost to be used in the future.

Program of Study – The student's declared major.

SAP – Satisfactory Academic Progress.

SAR – Student Aid Report.

Self-Help Aid – Financial aid that the student supplies himself or herself, such as savings, income, and loans.

SSN – Social Security number.

TIP – This acronym stand for Tuition Incentive Program. This program is a state-funded program for low-income students.

Tuition – The amount a college charges for classroom and other instruction.

Unmet Need – The amount of money you are short after taking into consideration your family help, scholarships, grants, loans, etc.

Verification – The process in which a student must verify all financial information given on their FAFSA forms.

Work Study – A financial-aid program that provides needy students with jobs throughout the school year.

CHAPTER 15

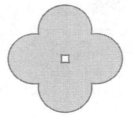

The Return to Normal

If you think that your life has changed quite a bit in the last few months, you have not seen anything yet. Being thrust into singlehood can be devastating, especially if your spouse dies or leaves unexpectedly. After handling the initial shock of your new lifestyle and finances, it is time to take a look at other decisions you now face to take back control of your life — and money.

Take a Good Look at Yourself

The first is coming to grips with the new you. No matter how hard you try not to change, this experience will undoubtedly change the way you think, feel, and even relate to those around you. This is a time to gain perspective on your life — the good and the bad. Maybe you feel guilty about not handling your spouse's illness "right," or you are still reeling from not understanding the role you may have played in the destruction of your marriage.

Take some time to look at your marriage as a whole to see the big picture. You may be surprised at what you discover. You did what you thought was right at the time, so do not double-guess yourself now. This experience has made you grow in ways you may have never thought possible and even if you would do things differently now that you have greater insight and knowledge does not mean you did anything wrong — just differently.

As for those who have survived a divorce — congratulations. You too walk away having gained a whole new understanding and appreciation for the wonderful person you are and what you can give to a relationship — and what you should stay clear of. Use this knowledge to prepare yourself for the next love interest coming your way. Whether it takes months or years to find another mate, you will be ready to accept love anew, free of the guilt and mistakes of the past.

Create a New Sense of Family

It does not matter if you have children or not: When you lose a spouse, you lose your sense of family. Of course, when children are involved, the importance of re-establishing that sense of family is heightened.

With so many changes in your life, you may be tempted to let go of old traditions and rituals in lieu of establishing brand new ones. Finding a way to make events and holidays special again without one of its main characters is important. You may not want to give up all of your old ways of doing things.

For instance, if your children have always looked forward to scouting a local tree farm for just the right Christmas tree, cutting it down themselves, and dragging it home, you may have to scale back a bit — going for a 5-foot tree instead of an 8-foot one — but consider still going out on your annual hunt. To suddenly forgo this important tradition for an artificial tree may be too much for you and your children to bear, despite your loss. However, if the mere thought of trying to find the perfect tree without your spouse is making the holidays unbearable, consider a compromise that you can all live with.

Of course, feel free to add some new rituals to your life in an attempt to make things normal again. One family who suffered a tragic loss reported that simply establishing a Friday night game-and-movie night helped bring them closer together after the death of their husband and father, and helped them reconnect as a family. This activity only proves that creating a new sense of family does not have to be difficult or cost a lot of money. The point here is to find ways to make everyone feel as if he or she still belongs and can survive whatever changes come his or her way.

Here are some ways you can help re-establish those family ties:

- Institute a family pizza night.
- Allow each member of the family to pick their favorite meal one night of the week.
- Choose a favorite vacation spot and go there every year for a while. This will offer small children continuity, which is important after a loss.
- Start a new hobby together.
- Spend time together having fun at least once a week.

Going Back to Work

Once you have started to reestablish a new family routine, you may find it necessary to re-enter the workforce, or change jobs to support yourself and your family on your own.

If it has been a while since you were in the workforce, you may be feeling a bit intimidated, not to mention a tad bit scared. After all, things may have changed a little — or changed a lot — in your profession since you last held down a full-time job. Or, like many women, you may have never been a "professional woman," and have no idea how to become one. Either way, there are a few things that you can do to help ease your way into the working world.

Step No. 1: Think About What You Want To Do

Now is not the time to grab at the first job that comes your way — unless, of course, you have to. Take some time to think about what you want to do and what type of career will best suit your new lifestyle. If you have small children and no support system, a position that requires a lot of overtime may not be your best option. However, a steady 9-to-5 job might work out just fine.

Think about what you like and do not like. After all, you will be spending a lot of time and energy at your new job; you might as well enjoy it as much as you can.

Next, think about your skills set. Do you have any special talents, skills, or training that can help you land the right job? If not, you may want to consider looking into some additional training or educational opportunities.

Step No. 2: Take a Catch-Up Course

You may need to brush up some of your skills, including on computer, or professional skills and certifications. Just about every industry has experienced changes in the last ten years, so if you have not been a part of it, you will likely need to take a few courses to get back on track.

Step No. 3: Outline a Job Search Strategy

Develop a solid network of people who can help you find the job you want and need. Think about your past business associates, or even people and places you have worked with in the past on a volunteer level. You never know who may know of a position that you would be a fit for. In the event that your spouse has died, you may even want to consider checking in with his or her last employer. He or she may be apt to give you an entry-level position in an area you are interested in.

Step No. 4: Brush Up On Your Interview Skills

If it has been a while since you were on a job interview, the first one or two may seem like torture. Use them as learning opportunities. And, if you simply are not sure how to interview at all, consider checking in with your local community college to see if it offers a course, seminar, workshop, or interviewing techniques through their job placement department. It is a way to learn new skills and practice them, too. Above all else, take any constructive feedback you hear to heart. Persistence pays. Remain upbeat, positive, and enthusiastic. The right attitude can open the doors you need to land a great job.

Step No. 5: Start With a Temporary Gig

A main key to landing the right job is simply getting noticed. Be open to any opportunity that comes your way, including temporary work. Taking a temp job is a good way to get your feet wet, see how you like a company or industry, or simply refresh some old skills. It is easier to land a temporary job than a permanent full-time one, yet it is a good way to get your foot in the door, make some contacts, and show your stuff.

Finding Your Passion:

Getting up and heading to work every day can be hard, but facing a job you hate can be pure hell. While you may need to "get a job" right away after your divorce or widowhood in order to pay the bills, you probably will want to begin thinking about what you really want to do with the rest of your life to find a fulfilling and worthwhile career that you cannot wait to get to every morning.

The first step in choosing the right career for you is finding your passion once again — something that can be much easier said than done after surviving such a traumatic experience. Here are some basic tips to get you started on your quest:

- **Get Curious** — Do not let any possibility slip through the cracks. Try looking at different jobs you would have never considered before. You never know when one might spark your interest.

- **Give Yourself a Deadline** — While you do not want to add stress to your life giving yourself a set of deadlines for investigating career choices; training opportunities and trying out new and interesting ideas can help push you forward toward a decision more quickly.

- **Find New Ways to Express Yourself** — This is a great way to figure out what you like, don't like, and give you an idea of how you would best like to spend your days.

- **Focus** — True, focusing might not be easy these days, but it is something you will have to relearn how to do if you want to find what you are good at and love once again.

- **Tap Into Your Talents** — Find ways to use your current skills and talents to create the career of your dreams.

- **Borrow Enthusiasm** — Enthusiasm is contagious, so why not borrow some from your friends and loved ones? Surround yourself with people who love what they do. Maybe their career choice is not what you are after, but taking some of their energy and passion may be just the jump-start you need to find your own pathway in the work world.

- **Break Free From The Chains** — When you are forced to do something — even something you like — you often begin to lose a passion for it. Remember, you always have a choice, so choose a job or career you can enjoy.

- **Find Some Confidence** — A lack of confidence will not only hold you back; it can snuff out any passion you may have. Do whatever is necessary to build enough confidence in your ability to give it a try. You may be surprised to discover you really are good at what you love most.

- **Enjoy the Hunt** — If the process of finding a passion is confusing to you, just play with it. You never know where a good hunt will lead.

Interviewing Tips

If your interviewing skills are a bit rusty, here are a few tips to get you started:

- Research the company before your big interview. Learn as much as you can about their products, services, management style, culture, dress code, and anything else you can think of.

- Do practice interviews with a career counselor, friends, and family members — or with yourself in front of a mirror.

- Think about how your previous experience — at work, school, or in your life — may benefit the company and enhance your work.

- Be early. Even if it means waiting in the lobby before heading to the interviewer's office, always be there in plenty of time — and never be late.

- Dress accordingly. Nothing makes a worse bad impression than wearing the wrong types of clothing for the job, such as casual work attire in a formal-attire office.

- Bring plenty of copies of your résumé

- Be sure to have a list of references ready

- Speak slowly and clearly

- Do not lie or exaggerate just to make a good impression

- Be assertive.

- Be sure to send a thank-you note right after the interview.

Dressing for Success

If there is one thing that no job seeker should underestimate, it is the power of dressing for success. No matter who you talk to, the facts are clear: The way you dress for an interview really does matter. According to the experts, as much as 55 percent of another person's perception of you is based on how you look.

How can you ensure that you are dressing correctly for your next interview? Follow these simple tips:

Women Should Wear:

- A conservative suit with a coordinated blouse
- Moderate shoes (no spiked heels)
- Basic jewelry
- A clean, professional-looking hairstyle
- Sparse make-up and perfume
- Manicured nails

Men Should Wear:

- A solid-colored conservative suit with a white dress shirt
- A plain conservative tie
- Dark socks and professional shoes
- A neat haircut

Where to Look for the Right Job

If it has been a few years since your last job hunt, you may be surprised at how much things have changed. Where once the classified ads in the local paper or a trip to the unemployment office may have garnered a long list of prospects, today's jobseekers have to be a bit savvier — and technologically sound. Here are a few of the most common places to look for a job in today's fast-paced world:

- **Internet Job Sites.** Sites such as **www.careerbuilders.com** or **www.monster.com** offer a quick way to see what is out there in the job world, and post your résumé, as well as apply for specific positions online.

- **Job Fairs.** An effective way to see what companies in your area are hiring and what positions are available, as well as an opportunity to meet with job makers face to face, job fairs can offer a variety of opportunities in a one-stop shop atmosphere.

- **Job Placement Agencies.** If you offer specific skills, you may want to consider finding an agency that caters to that industry. Of course, there will be a fee for their services.

- **Recruitment Firms.** If you are in the market for a relatively high-level position, a recruitment firm may be the answer, as most mid- to high-range positions in larger corporations are hired this way.

- **Associates.** Let everyone you come in contact with know that you are job hunting. The people we know are our best ally in finding a position or landing that all-important interview.

- **Company Web sites.** Have a certain job, company, or industry in mind? Check out individual company Web sites for job postings.

Going Back to School

Depending on how long you have been out of the job market, or what industry you would like to look for a job in, you may need to go back to school for the education/certification you will need.

Assuming that you already know what you want to study, the bigger question may be its affordability. College is expensive, and finding a way to pay for it in addition to your other bills may seem at out the question, at first. But there is hope. In addition to student loans and grants, adult students find a wealth of financing options, including some that traditional students do not qualify for.

Employer-Financed Tuition

If you are already working, you may be able to get help from your employer. Many employers these days offer tuition aid for any program, as long as it is at an accredited school. Your company's human resources department will have all the details. But, here are a few things to watch out for:

- **What Level of Reimbursement is Available?** Some companies are willing to foot the entire bill, while others only pay a percentage of tuition fees.

- **What Grades They Require to Qualify for Reimbursement?** Most employers require student-employees to have at least a B or higher grade point average to qualify.

- **When Payment is Made.** Some employers make tuition reimbursements when you register for a class; others when you are finished and have proof of a passing grade; and still others may pay only on an annual or semi-annual basis, leaving you to lay out initial costs and wait for reimbursement.

Home Equity Loans/Lines of Credit

If you have equity in your home, you may be able to tap into it to pay those college bills. An equity loan will require taking all the money you need at once and paying it back monthly from the date the loan is approved, while a line of credit allows you to take the money as you need it, which will make your payments much lower in the beginning.

Retirement Savings

Most retirement plans will allow the holder to borrow interest-free money for tuition and pay it back at your leisure.

Military Assistance

If you or your deceased spouse was ever in the military, you may qualify for tuition assistance through a variety of programs. The most common include:

- **Tuition Assistance Programs:** Designed to give the current full-time, full-duty military personnel a chance to earn their degree while still serving. Tuition Assistance Programs give military personnel up to 100-percent per fiscal year for college costs. Look here for more information: **www.military.com/money-for-school/tuition-assistance/tuition-assistance-ta-program-overview**

- **Montgomery G.I. Bill:** The most well-known of the military's tuition programs, the G.I. Bill will pay as much as $37,000 toward college costs after completing a three-year commitment in full-time duty. One downfall to this program is that military personnel must sign up for and contribute $100 per month to the program for one year in order to qualify.

- **College Fund Programs:** In addition to the G.I. Bill, those serving full-time in the military may also qualify for an additional $30,000 or more in aid, depending on the branch they belong to.

- **Loan Repayment Programs:** Each branch of the military offers its own unique form of this program, with its own requirements and loan reimbursement limits, but all offer some type of loan repayment programs for those who have served.

Scholarships

Depending on your circumstances, there may be a scholarship available. Many charities and non-profit organizations and foundations now offer myriad scholarship options for the adult student — especially women and single mothers. Two helpful Web sites that can give you an idea of the scholarship help available to adults nationally are **www.charitywire.com** and **www.cof.org**. Do not forget to check out those smaller, local charities too. They might offer scholarships through partnerships with local philanthropists.

Going Back to School the Modern Way

Going to college sure has changed over the years. Gone are the days when you had to sit at those half desks for hours, listening to a boring lecture. Today's student plugs into the Internet at his or her leisure, attends class, and hands in assignments, all online. It can be great news for someone who needs to juggle home, work, and schoolwork.

Finding a good program is not all that hard if you keep these things in mind:

- Look for one that offers the same class work and instruction as on-site classes
- Make sure it offers regular contact methods with the professor and other classmates
- Check to make sure that it uses the same basic textbooks as the on-site courses

Of course, going to school online is not always easy; the simple fact is that some students need a classroom setting to succeed. But if you are good at learning independently, and a traditional college experience simply is not in the cards right now, give online learning a try. It just may be what you need.

Things to Ask Yourself When Considering an Online Education

Although there are great benefits to studying from home via Internet, online education does have its drawbacks: It can be difficult to connect with other students, ask on-the-spot questions, or even stay on track.

Studying online is not easy, and it is not for everyone. So how do you know if going after an online degree is the right choice for you? Ask yourself these important questions:

1. **Am I Self-Motivated?** When you are involved in online education, you must be your own self-motivator. If you cannot stay on track without a professor in a classroom environment day after day, you may want to consider a more traditional college option.

2. **What is My Personal Learning Style?** Taking college courses online can be difficult for auditory learners who must hear and see lectures firsthand. Some classes may be viewed via taped lectures and watched on your computer screen, but others may only be written professor's notes. It all depends on the program you choose and the way the individual professor decided to handle teaching the actual course. However, people who find it hard to sit in a classroom for a one- to three-hour lecture may find the ability to watch the lecture again and again helpful in learning and studying the material. Understanding your own personal learning style will help you better choose the school, program, and online classes you will need to complete your degree.

3. **How Flexible is My Schedule?** The nice thing about many online courses is that they offer the flexibility to log on at your convenience, regardless of the time or day.

4. **Is the Program I am Interested in Conducive to Online Learning?** Some degree programs are more conducive to this type of academic freestyle learning than others. An accountant major, for instance, can learn everything he or she needs to know from books, making an online degree simple and easy to get. Becoming a nurse, however, requires hours outside a classroom, which cannot be attained through an online class. Make sure you thoroughly understand the limitations of obtaining your online degree and be sure you know how clinical studies will be handled.

5. **Can I Complete My Entire Degree Online?** Some schools allow you to finish your entire degree online, while others require classroom attendance for a portion of your studies.

As you can see, there are many things to consider when deciding whether to take an online course. Be sure you consider all of the pros and cons to an online education before taking the plunge into this modern way of going to college.

The Pitfalls of Online Learning

Online education has opened the floodgates of opportunity for many students who might otherwise never be able to attend college and earn their degree. But, it does not come without its pitfalls.

Pitfall No. 1: Not All Online Programs Are Alike

There are a lot of good online programs out there — and a lot of not-so-good ones, too. Here are a few things to look at when choosing the program that is right for you:

- If it is accredited by a national accreditation organization/school
- If it allows you to transfer online credits to a more traditional programs and/or schools
- If it offers the same type of classes and basic education as its traditional students receive
- If it offers the same degree as the school's traditional students receive
- If it is accepted by other schools and employers

Pitfall No. 2: Watch Out For Accelerated Schedules

It may sound like a good idea to finish your degree in half the time, until you realize that it will take twice the work in half the time to complete each class. This can be a difficult schedule to keep, especially if you have not been a student for a while — if ever.

Pitfall No. 3: Not All Programs Can Be Completed Online

Be sure that your entire program can be completed online, especially if it is not possible to attend classes on the college campus. Some online colleges programs require students to do some of their coursework on-site at their local campus. Be sure you understand the limitations of the program you seek.

Pitfall No. 4: Some Programs Do Not Qualify for Financial Aid

Even online programs offered at reputable colleges do not always qualify for financial aid packages. Talk with your school's financial aid office to be certain that classes taken online qualify in the same manner for financial aid help as their traditional classes.

Pitfall No. 5: Not Everyone is a Good Candidate for Distance Learning

Most people think they would excel if left on their own, but the fact remains that it takes an organized self-motivator to be able to do an entire college degree practically on his or her own. Depending on your individual learning style, you may need to have the ability to ask on-the-spot questions during a lecture, or be able to talk with other students after class. However, if you do not need that one-on-one kind of attention to get work done, then by all means consider this type of flexible learning.

Connecting with the Outside World Again

It may be hard to fathom right now, in the midst of your pain, but someday you will be ready to jumpstart your social life again. Maybe that will entail getting out there and meeting new people, or finding new interests that you can do alone, or maybe it will mean looking for love all over again. Either way, it is important to remember that we all can benefit from a connection with others.

Re-entering the world of singles can be both scary and frustrating. After all, it probably has been a long time since you have had to find things to do on your own. If you dislike dining alone, then call old friends and invite them to dinner at your favorite restaurant. If you do not want to feel like a third wheel because all of your friends are coupled up, join a singles group at your church or community center and meet some new friends. There are plenty of other singles out there facing the same obstacles that you are, and many would love to find someone to do things with on a social level.

Some simple ways to reconnect with the outside world include:

- Take a non-credit or adult enrichment course
- Join a reading, hobby, or some other social club
- Start doing something completely new that has always interested you
- Join a singles group
- Learn a new sport/join a team
- Go places you have never been before (a museum, an art gallery)
- Do not be afraid to strike up a conversation with someone new

When it is time to start dating again, you may be surprised at how things have changed since you were last on the playing field. The most common ways that today's singles find love include:

- **Online Dating Services.** We have all seen the commercials of lonely singles finding love on the Internet. While these services may not offer the love connection their commercials tout, they are a good place to begin meeting new people and regain your dating style.

- **Their Friends.** Let the people in your life know that you are dating again. The odds are they have someone in mind. After all, these are the people who know you best and have first-hand insight into your likes and dislikes.

- **Groups.** Singles groups are a great way to meet other singles in your area and offer a variety of social opportunities to get to know a wide range of people.

- **Charities.** Volunteering for a local charity that is dear to your heart can open up a whole new world of dating prospects. Consider this: You have a lot in common with someone who also has taken the time and energy to give their time to charity you also believe in.

- **Personal Ads.** Sure, you may have made fun of those desperate souls in the past, but consider how many people have found true love through a variety of personal ads. What do you have to lose but some postage and a little time reading through the responses you will likely get?

- **Speed Dating.** In this fast-paced world, finding a date has also turned high-speed. Speed dating offers the opportunity to meet a dozen or more people in one evening, thus giving you multiple opportunities to make a good first impression and find someone you may connect with.

Tips for Using an Online Dating Service Safely:

It can be a scary world out there, and whether you are meeting people online or face-to-face, it is important to take precautions to ensure your safety. Here are a few tips to use when looking for love via the Internet:

1. **Never Give Your Personal Information In Your Profile.** Be careful about who you give your personal information to, including your address, phone number, or your personal e-mail address until you have had ample opportunity to get to know him or her and are sure he or she is *safe*.

2. **Never Use Your Private E-mail Address.** Even if you decide to leave the online service for communication, set up an anonymous e-mail account to help safeguard your privacy.

3. **Take Multiple Precautions When Meeting in Person**. If you decide to finally meet the person you have been corresponding with in-person, be sure to take multiple precautions, such as driving yourself to the rendezvous point, meeting in a public place, driving to a friend's home afterward in case you are followed, telling someone where you are going and who you will be with, or taking along a friend for support.

4. **Consider Running a Background Check On Anyone You Meet Online**. It may sound a bit daunting to have to check out every person you decide to communicate with, but you cannot be too careful. There are a lot of unscrupulous people out there who prey on innocent people trying to simply find someone to love. Be sure that you take care of both your physical self as well as your emotional self when dating online.

Getting Remarried

If finding a new love seems impossible right now, the thought of remarrying may leave an even nastier taste in your mouth. The fact remains that two-thirds of all divorcées and widows and widowers do remarry within the first ten years of becoming single once again.

Considering those statistics, the odds seem in your favor of finding a new spouse sometime down the line. That may leave you with a lot to think about in regards to your financial future, as well as your emotional one. If you do not have children, it may be easier to accept a new love into your life. However, when children are involved, you need to take special care to protect their interests — especially when it comes to your money.

When considering remarrying, take into account what you may be giving up. In most cases, any Social Security benefits you were receiving will cease; the ability to claim your ex-spouse's Social Security benefit levels will no longer apply; and in most cases, any alimony set forth in your divorce decree will stop. Ask yourself this important question: Is it worth it? For some, the answer may be an overwhelming yes, while for others, the losses they will incur may not seem worth the risk of taking on a new spouse.

Consider a Pre-Nuptial Agreement

Rich or poor, requiring your new spouse to sign a prenuptial agreement is a good idea, especially if you have any amount of assets at all.

If you have already survived one divorce, you fully understand the emotional and financial upheaval it can cause in your life. With no guarantees that your new marriage will fare any better than your old one, a prenuptial agreement can help you safeguard your finances should things go awry in the future.

Although it may seem a bit cynical to consider the possibility of failure before you have even given your new marriage a try, the truth of the matter is that nearly 75 percent of remarriages fail. You should be prepared.

A prenuptial agreement is not a sign that you do not trust your new mate, or that you intend to dissolve the marriage in the future; but it does allow you to ensure that what you bring into the marriage remains yours (and yours alone), should the situation turn nasty.

There are a lot of reasons why a pre-nuptial agreement is a good idea, including:

- The ability to make a split easier and cheaper

- The ability to protect business assets from your previous marriage — or those you have built since becoming single again
- The ability to protect any money you have inherited or earned on your own
- The ability to protect your children's rightful inheritance
- The ability to negotiate the terms of your marriage, including who will be responsible for what costs, duties, etc.

Not always just about money, many modern couples use this type of pre-marriage agreement to establish certain rules for their marriage. This is especially popular for those who have undergone nasty divorces in the past and may include such topics as:

- Whether they will have children
- Whether one of you will stay home to care for minor children
- How you will handle the parenting responsibilities regarding children from previous marriages
- How you will handle combined debt
- How much you will save
- Whether you will have a joint or individual bank accounts
- How you will share housework

No matter how justified you may feel in asking your new mate to sign a prenuptial agreement, the fact remains that it can still cause a rift between the best of couples. The most important thing to stress when broaching this emotional subject is that it is not based on mistrust, but rather a feeling of security. No matter what, be honest. Try to explain why you feel the need to ask for a prenuptial agreement and be clear what you want it to include (and exclude). Maybe you simply want a legal document that safeguards your home for your children, or find it necessary to exclude your new spouse from business decisions, if your deceased spouse started the business. Those are legitimate concerns and need to be addressed. Just be sure you do so in an honest, loving, and clear manner. Avoid becoming defensive or angry. After all, you are the one asking for special circumstances here, and need to show some strong understanding as to your new mate's feelings.

Making It Legal

When wiring a prenuptial agreement, be sure it is legal. Here are some simple tips to follow to ensure it will hold up in court should the need arise:

1. Make sure everything is in writing. If it is not written down, there is no way to prove that your spouse agreed to it.

2. The document must be signed by both partners and notarized.

3. The document should be discussed, outlined, and signed well before the wedding date to ensure that a court does not make it null and void due to an appearance of coercion.

4. Both partners must be 100 percent honest about their assets at the time of the marriage. If a court finds that either of you hid certain facts about their wealth (or debt), or tried to minimize the value of certain assets, they can see fit to declare the document invalid.

To avoid any legal hassles in the future, it is always a good idea to have any prenuptial agreement drafted and held by an attorney.

Moving on with your life after a death or divorce is never easy, and sometimes it can make entering into a new marriage more difficult. But that does not mean love is out of the question now or in the future. What it does mean is that your experiences now will affect the way you handle relationships in the future and may make the practicalities of building a life together more important the second time around.

Dating Tips:

Stepping back out into the dating field can be hard, especially if it has been awhile since you were single. So, here are some dating tips to get you started on this new journey for love — or maybe just companionship:

- Decide who and what you want. Know what you are looking for and do some research on where to find it.

- Get your act together. Start working out. Buy some new clothes. Get a new hairstyle. Start looking your best.

- Set some goals. Decide what your dating goals are. Do you want to find someone to do things with, or do you want a long-term relationship? Be clear what you want — with yourself and those you date — to make the most of each dating experience.

- Look in all the right places. Hanging out with your married friends at their backyard BBQs may not yield many prospects, yet going to a new bar every Friday night might showcase the wrong kind of attention. Find some neutral singles haunts like the local museum, library, shows, restaurants, and more to meet new folk.

- Enjoy the process. Remember, dating does not require a permanent love connection, but rather allows you to test the waters a bit and get to know a lot of different types of people to see what sparks your interest.

- Do not make yourself too available. People like mystery and the thrill of the chase when dating.

Successful Dating Is...

What makes a date successful? Here are a few ideas to contemplate:

- Finding someone with similar interests and values
- Establishing dating boundaries
- Being upbeat — no one wants to date a downer
- Keeping things simple and lighthearted (at least at the beginning)

- Being flexible
- Being realistic about your expectations
- Allowing yourself to loosen up and have fun

Dating with Confidence

Not sure how to start dating again — or if you should? Here are a few confidence builders to help get you ready for that first big date:

- First, ask yourself if you want to meet someone new, or if you think you should because of what others are saying. If the time is not now, then hold off until you *are* ready.

- Make a list of all the things you do not like about yourself. Try and change any bad habits for better ones.

- Give yourself a makeover: new hair, clothes, new makeup. Forget what everyone else will think and say. Do what feels right to you.

- Shake up your normal routine. That is a great way to feel more confident.

- Get yourself on a healthy diet and exercise program. If you are not taking the best care of your body, you will not be able to feel good about yourself.

- Start doing the things you wish you had always had the courage to do. Maybe start a hobby or sport, or join a club or social society such as the Rotary, Kiwanis, or others.

- Learn to enjoy the smaller things in life and give yourself time to enjoy the world around you.

- Start putting yourself first — you deserve it.

- Set some life goals not associated with any romantic notions you may be harboring. Confidence comes from within.

- Be proactive. Do not wait for someone else to ask you out — try doing the asking yourself. He or she just might say yes. And, if he or she does not, try someone else.

- Learn to like and love yourself for who you are and what you want from your life. Learn to make conversation with the people you meet along the way.

- Be friendly and open.

- Be persistent. Meeting new people might be hard, but it is worth the effort.

Helping Your Kids Adjust to Your New Love Interest

Some kids do not seem to care when their divorced parents start dating again, and others take it hard — very hard. So, when is the right time to introduce your children to your new love interest? Most experts agree that later is better than sooner.

First, be sure that your children have gotten over the divorce before bringing a new man or woman into the picture. Give them time to grieve the life they once knew and come to grips with their new reality.

Secondly, make sure that your new relationship is solid before upsetting the delicate balance you and your children have come to achieve since the death of your spouse or your divorce. There is no use in upsetting everyone for a quick fling that is over before it ever had the chance to begin.

Finally, when making those first important impressions, make it casual: An accidental meeting at a restaurant, or a trip to the park. Never try to push your new love interest on your children. Give them time to inspect the new love in your life and sort out their own thoughts and emotions. And never let them spend the night if your children are the least bit leery or upset over you dating anyone at all. This will only cause further conflict and may create a wedge between you, your children, and your new date that may take months to heal —if ever.

No matter what the circumstances are, or how old your children are, it can be difficult for them to admit that you are moving on and that the life you once shared as a family is indeed over for good. Give them time and be patient. Otherwise, you risk more stress and a broken relationship amongst you all.

One Final Thought...

You opened this book with the hopes of learning something to help you get through the most difficult transition of your life: living without your spouse. Within its pages, you have learned how to prepare for the worst; take a good hard look at your financial situation; budget your finances according to your new income; get the insurance you need; plan for your financial future; get a job; and even start over.

We hope that this guide has helped you find the answers to the questions that may have left you stumped before picking it up. Although we tried our best to be as comprehensive as possible, you may find yourself with lingering questions in need of a few answers. If this is the case, check out the Resource Rolodex in the Appendices for a listing of organizations and Web sites that may be of further assistance.

In addition to the practical help offered, we want to wish every one of our readers the best that life has to offer. It has certainly been a rough road to travel together, but remember: You are a survivor. You have made it this far and you will make it through the rest of your journey. Whether you are just beginning in this new life path, or you have been on your own a while now, always know that you have made it this far, and there will be better days ahead. Watch for it — it is surely headed your way. Good luck to you all.

APPENDICES

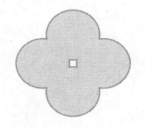

APPENDIX A:

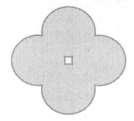

Case Studies

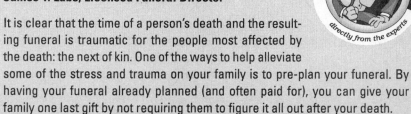

CASE STUDY 1: THE IMPORTANCE OF PRE-PLANNING YOUR FUNERAL

McCune Garden Chapel
212 Main St.
Vacaville, CA
James T. Lubs, Licensed Funeral Director

It is clear that the time of a person's death and the result-
ing funeral is traumatic for the people most affected by
the death: the next of kin. One of the ways to help alleviate
some of the stress and trauma on your family is to pre-plan your funeral. By
having your funeral already planned (and often paid for), you can give your
family one last gift by not requiring them to figure it all out after your death.

One common misconception about pre-paid funerals, however, is that it will
lock in the prices, thus making your final arrangements cheaper. The benefits
of prepaying for a funeral can vary from state to state. In theory, prepaying for
a funeral *should* be the vehicle for locking in the price for merchandise and
the services to be rendered by the funeral home of your choice, with any an-
cillary charges being covered by the interest that accrues over time on your
account, but this is not always the case. Be sure you clearly understand what
you are prepaying for, so as not to cost your family more after your death.
And, in some rare cases, you may actually pay more now than your family
would have in the future. This has been the case in some areas of the country
where the cost of cremation has declined in recent years. Still, the benefits of

CASE STUDY 1: THE IMPORTANCE OF PRE-PLANNING YOUR FUNERAL

handling these preparations seem to outweigh any disadvantages.

So, when is the best time to preplan your funeral? For most, it is advisable to make your arrangements well in advance of a time where you suspect an impending need. An excellent opportunity for such planning is the same time that you are setting up preparations for the handling of your estate. You do not have to be elderly or facing a life-threatening illness in order to write out your plans. As a matter of fact, it is best to be prepared and take on the planning aspect while in a healthy condition, with an open-minded approach that exercises sound judgment.

There are numerous matters to be considered while planning your estate, and I deem it only appropriate to treat the disposition of your remains with greater importance than the disposition of your finances.

Preplanning for the funeral has the relative merits of having your very personal plans carried out as you wish and gives you the knowledge that family members will be relieved of the stress that accompanies such decision-making. This is a process that is arguably considered one of the most demanding and traumatic events one endures while on this planet.

How to Ensure That Your Family Can Afford Your Burial

When most people think of preplanning their funeral, they think about buying a casket, determining the style and tone of the service, and even making arrangements for a family meal following the burial. But one does not always need to make such detailed arrangements in regard to his or her funeral.

One of the biggest obstacles families face during this traumatic time is finding the money needed to pay for the arrangements. One important way to ensure that your family is prepared financially for your death and funeral is to invest the funds needed in a regulated trust, a life insurance policy, or even establish a savings account or certificate of deposit that is earmarked solely for your funeral expenses.

But remember, in today's fast-paced, ever-changing world, it is not uncommon for a family to find themselves relocating. It is important to know whether the account is transferable. Not all accounts are portable, while many insurance policies are. Be sure that you understand any limitations any account you open may have.

CASE STUDY 2: STAYING PRACTICAL IN THE MIDST OF CHAOS

Michelle Deery Thomas, widow
Nationwide Insurance
35 S. High Street
West Chester, PA 19380
610-696-6560

Michelle, now the owner of a successful insurance agency, knows first-hand how important preparation and being sufficiently insured can be in the case of the loss of a spouse.

Although she and her husband were aware of his health condition and had time to prepare for his death, she still had the responsibility of caring for and subsequently providing for six children. As a widow at the age of 38, with children 4, 10, 11, 17, 18, and 19 years old, she was probably more prepared than the average person because her husband was an insurance agent and had been teaching her the business for years.

His health condition had made him uninsurable ten years before his death — something most people don't consider when they are young and don't yet have life insurance. Many people don't want to think about the possibility of losing a spouse, but the reality is that without considering it, you may find yourself horribly unprepared.

She advises all her clients who have young families to have enough life insurance to cover both the breadwinner and the caregiver. Otherwise, if the breadwinner should pass away and the other parent not be adequately insured, the children would essentially lose both parents as their primary caregiver would have to find a way to support the family. Having adequate life insurance can allow the widow or widower to concentrate on putting their life back together, grieving, and caring for their children instead of worrying about how to put food on the table.

In hindsight, Michelle feels she could have done some things differently, such as talking more with her late husband about how she felt, and showing her children more of her own vulnerability. However, the financial and insurance planning they put into place enabled Michelle to survive the short term. She was able to keep her house and raise her children without the extra burden of extreme financial crisis. Now, she is thriving with her own insurance business.

Helping Your Spouse Die Without Fear

There's no right way to help your spouse die. But if there's one piece of advice that I would share with others going through this horrible ordeal, it is to listen more. Michelle urges others facing the same circumstances that she has already lived with (and through):

CASE STUDY 2: STAYING PRACTICAL IN THE MIDST OF CHAOS

"I wish I had tried to listen to my husband a little more. He wanted to talk about his impending death — to share his feelings — but I was so busy trying to encourage him and to think positively, I failed to listen to his fears. If I could do things differently, I would have tried better to balance desire to have him not be negative and my desire to be his sounding board.

That's not to say we ignored what was happening. We did talk extensively about what was coming and what he wanted, and we had many conversations. But every so often he would make an off-handed remark, which I could have responded to better."

There is no manual for the sorrow, or for handling those feelings of pending doom and the sadness you feel while trying your best to value every moment you have left. You just do the best you can and try to make memories that will help you get through it all later. Sometimes, listening can be the memories that sustain you for years to come.

Dealing With Your Grief Your Way

"There are no 'shoulds' when it comes to surviving your spouse's death. You should do whatever you feel like doing. Don't let people tell you that you have to clean out the closet of his clothes. If those clothes, their smell, their presence gives you one second of comfort, then leave them until the day the spirit moves you... and then you will do what needs to be done.

Everyone, including children, move through this process at different rates of speed. Some are in denial, while another might be really angry, while another is deeply depressed. As the parent, you have to try to balance each child's place in the process while you are grieving as well. I used to sit in the closet at night with his bathrobe and sob...I didn't want the kids to see me because I was afraid they would be afraid. My one child now tells me she never saw me cry... and she sort of says it with an edge...so I think I maybe should have let them see me *not* be the rock I apparently gave them the impression I was. One of the biggest surprises I uncovered after my husband's death was that I began to thrive once he was gone. When I was no longer involved with his dying, I began to reinvest in myself a little bit. When he died, I began to flourish just due to the reinvestment of energy from taking care of him to taking care of myself.

It was interesting because women become suspicious of you when you are widowed and looking like you are doing okay. But, like I said earlier, there aren't any 'shoulds' in surviving. Just do what feels right and you'll be OK."

CASE STUDY 3: DIVORCE

H&R Block
707 Boston Post Rd
Old Saybrook, CT 06475
(860) 388-0360
Margaret Shepard – (Old Saybrook H&R Block)

The major tax change implication that you should be aware of after either a divorce or the death of your spouse is that of filing status. The benefit you receive is contingent on the status with which you file.

Divorce

The year prior to the divorce, you may still file married joint or may choose to file married separated. Careful consideration of your options and the full weight of their impact on your bottom line is a valuable step to take before deciding what status to file. Filing as separated while you are married is considered to be an unfavorable filing status. You should have strong financial reason when opting for this status. Perhaps your spouse is engaged in or owns a business in which you do not want to be a responsible party with regard to the filing of his taxes. Given such circumstances, one spouse may not want to share in the responsibility of signing the same tax form with their soon-to-be ex-partner. Be aware that along with electing the married filing separate status, you will forfeit a lot of the credits you would otherwise be entitled to (in regard to) for children.

Once the divorce has taken place by December 31, you must file with a status of Not Married. "Not" is the keyword in respect to the IRS. You may still have choices in regard to filing status. Filing as single is one option, and if there is a child or children that resides with you six months plus one day out of the year, you may be able to file Head of Household. With this status comes a lower tax rate.

Keep in mind that divorce is a matter of choice; although it may not have been what you had in mind, it is still considered a choice, unlike the death of a spouse.

Death of a Spouse

This is not a matter of choice, but rather of unfortunate circumstance. The year following the death of a spouse is an emotional one, to say the least. Your finances, and in turn your income taxes, are just two of the areas impacted by this life-changing event. It can be overwhelming, and you may find some relief in the tax benefit that is provided. For the year in which the death occurred,

CASE STUDY 3: DIVORCE

the surviving spouse may still file their tax return with a status of married filing jointly on the return. This buys a good amount of time to do planning. The exception, although rare, is when the surviving spouse remarries within the same year in which their spouse became deceased.

This means that you for that first year you will retain:

- Filing status
- Exemption status (even 65 or older)
- Deductions when filing joint
- Tax rate when filing joint

After the death of a spouse, there are many changes that impact or change the amount of your income and thus have bearing on the income taxes you file. If you were both collecting Social Security, you will now be collecting one check instead of two. You will get an amount equal to the larger of the two checks, but this still has a negative impact on your cash flow.

Pensions are another area that may affect your income. A pension with survivor payments will continue to provide income. In the case of a pension that was selected without choosing the survivorship option, then the income from the pension will cease. Income from investments will remain the same, while an IRA can be rolled over into the surviving spouse's IRA until the time in which they become 70.5 years of age. Therefore, the money in the IRA does not have a huge tax consequence.

If you are a widow or widower with dependent children, then you may well be eligible to get a two-year tax break. As a qualifying widow or widower, you may be able to file with a status of qualifying widow or widower with dependent child on your tax return. This status allows you to use the joint return tax rates, and if don't itemize the highest standard deduction amount. Keep in mind that standard deductions will apply not deceased person exemptions. After this two-year period, a widow or widower may file Head of Household, which is considered a favorable tax status.

Take a deep breath… the first year is not much different than the year before. Talk with a tax specialist about how to prepare for the future changes that will impact your taxes. You may want to make estimated payments toward any expected increase in your taxes in advance of filing the final return. One of the most significant benefits offered is the advantage this time offers to prepare for the year ahead.

CASE STUDY 4: LILI A. VASILEFF

Lili A. Vasileff
Certified Financial Planner®
Certified Divorce Financial Analyst™
Registered Investment Advisor
President of the Association of Divorce Financial Planners
Two Sound View Drive, Suite 100
Greenwich, CT 06830
www.divorcematters.com
203-622-4911 and 203-393-7200

I was a newly divorced mother of two small children, sitting outside my 5-year-old son's therapist's office. My son was excited and looked remarkably calm, when the therapist suggested to me that perhaps it might be a good idea for me to join the adult group that met simultaneously. Sitting through that discussion group, I was dumbfounded to learn that most women going through divorce were floundering over their finances, out of fear, lack of experience, or lack of proper and helpful advice.

This is when the lights went on. I was encouraged and inspired to fill the obvious need for providing accurate financial advocacy and analysis to individuals going through divorce. It has now been 15 years since I left the corporate world to start my own divorce financial planning business. Over the years, I have discovered financial expertise is a blessing to those trying to navigate a legal process that results in financial decisions that last a lifetime. Each case is unique, but there are similar themes that pop up.

The main things that newly divorced or widowed persons should consider include drafting a new will, a living will, a health care proxy, and maybe even legal/financial guardian papers for minor children. On the financial end, one should designate beneficiaries on all accounts, set up an emergency fund equal to three to six months worth of fixed expenses, invest regularly for themselves, monitor spending to pay bills on time and maintain a good credit score, and lastly, maximize retirement savings, especially those plans where employers match your contributions.

On the dark side, common pitfalls exist for the newly single person, such as thinking someone else will take care of them financially in the future; assuming money is too hard to understand; investing is too risky; or that it is too late to start saving in any meaningful way. The single most important piece of advice I give to newly single persons is to start saving regularly for their retirement. Saving should be a required monthly expense, as any other. The compounding value of money is always surprising, and it is never too late. I also suggest protecting yourself in every way against accumulating too many

CASE STUDY 4: LILI A. VASILEFF

credit cards, consumer fraud, and identity theft. You may be vulnerable to new deals, offers, solicitations — and being inexperienced with finances, do not fall prey. Know what identity information is absolutely required, and require service providers to protect your private information.

A good financial planner is your ally for evaluating your lifestyle; assisting you with making financial improvements; identifying new goals; and helping you secure resources such as mortgages, life insurance, long-term care insurance, and investment advice. You should aim to work with a Certified Financial Planner and get recommendations from friends, family, and colleagues. During a divorce, you should aim to work with a divorce financial planner trained in the interdisciplinary nature of law and finance in your state. A divorce financial planner is a unique financial expert who can help you assess your lifestyle needs, negotiate settlements, analyze tax consequences, and provide long-term projections of where you will be financially post-divorce, given various legal scenarios. You can find divorce financial planners at **www.divorceandfinance.org**.

Without a good financial planner on your side, you can easily make big mistakes, like spending your lump sum settlement instead of investing it for your future; getting into too much debt and damaging your credit worthiness; finding yourself locked into expenses without any emergency or liquid funds when the unexpected happens; not knowing if you should be filing quarterly taxes or drawing down from IRA accounts; and the biggest one: failing to plan for the long term because it is too scary or intangible. The challenge to become financially secure and knowledgeable is to take advantage of all possible resources that promote your self-esteem and responsible behavior with money.

Lili Vasileff is the President of the Association of Divorce Financial Planners, the largest national not-for-profit organization of divorce financial planners and allied divorce professionals. She is a fee-only Certified Financial Planner and is a nationally recognized expert in financial planning for divorce as a practitioner, writer, and speaker. Her Web site is **www.divorcematters.com**. Vasileff has many years of experience and an interdisciplinary knowledge of legal and financial issues. She brings clarity to complicated marital property and complex compensation issues in the divorce process. She supports divorcing clients in mediation, collaborative divorce, and litigation in Connecticut and New York. Starting more than 15 years ago, Vasileff was a pioneer in this field, which she began as a result of her own experience as a divorced mother of two young children and based on her passion to promote financial justice in the divorce process. She was named as one of the Top Financial Planners of 2008 by Consumers' Research Council of America and has received numerous other honors and awards for service and pro bono work.

CASE STUDY 5: CREDIT MATTERS

Lisa C. Decker, CDFA
Lisa@DivorceMoneyMatters.com
Divorce Financial Insight, LLC
Divorce Money Matters
www.DivorceMoneyMatters.com
PO Box 65
Kennesaw, Ga. 30152
Phone: 866-722-7226

This is an area I see many people make mistakes in because they don't realize even if their divorce decree gives a debt to their ex-spouse and makes their ex-spouse accountable for paying it, courts have no jurisdiction over creditors in accepting that settlement and agreement.

Divorce courts do not have the power to wipe out your obligations to lenders, such as credit cards, auto loans, or mortgage companies. If your name is still attached to a debt, then you are still liable for it, even if your spouse has been the one ordered to pay that debt.

Take the case of Linda and Tom. Linda and I met through a friend at a party after her divorce had been finalized. Unfortunately, the story she shared with me is all too common.

This couple didn't have a lot of assets or debts and thought that their situation was fairly simple. They used one attorney to draw up the papers, as the divorce was uncontested.

Here's how it panned out (Numbers have been rounded and adjusted for simplicity's sake):

Linda		Joint	Tom	
House	$150,000	$150,000		
Mortgage debt	($125,000)	($125,000)		
½ Investments	$50,000	$100,000	$50,000	½ Investments
		$75,000	$75,000	401(k)
Her car	$10,000	$30,000	$20,000	His car
Her car loan	($10,000)	($30,000)	($20,000)	His car loan
		($50,000)	($50,000)	Credit card debt
Net to wife	**$75,000**	**$150,000**	**$75,000**	**Net to husband**

CASE STUDY 5: CREDIT MATTERS

Linda kept the house and the mortgage obligation, half their investments, and her car, along with the car loan associated with it. Tom kept his 401(k), half the investments, his car along with the car loan associated with it, and assumed all of the credit card debt.

Within six months, Tom lost his job and quickly went through his savings. When he couldn't pay the credit card debt, the late charges and interest began to accrue. To make matters go from bad to worse, the credit card companies skyrocketed his interest rates from 9.99 percent to 27.99 percent because he now had become more of a credit risk.

Meanwhile, Linda had no idea that her credit was going down the tubes as well because her name was still on all those joint credit cards. She hadn't concerned herself with any of this because he was the one the court had ordered to make the payments, and he was receiving the statements.

In the meantime, Linda also began experiencing financial troubles because she soon realized the house was more than she could afford on her own. This is a common mistake I see many women make because they are emotionally attached to the home. She also went through her savings during this time.

When Linda decided that she would try to refinance to lower her rate and potentially take some of the equity from the home, what she found out was devastating. Because of Tom's troubles with the still-joint credit cards, her credit had also taken a nosedive, and she was no longer a candidate for refinancing.

Within a few months, she lost the home to foreclosure, which in turn only made Tom's situation worse, as his name was still on the mortgage, as well.

Unfortunately, now both parties find their credit is ruined, and it will take them years to rebuild.

Better Scenario:

Had Linda and I met before her divorce, I would have given her some pre-divorce planning advice that would have made her aware of the dangers of their scenario.

My recommendations might have been to organize this scenario:

- Sell the home and split the equity and each buy something smaller and more affordable, or rent for a while.

CASE STUDY 5: CREDIT MATTERS

- Jointly agree to pay off the credit card debts, close those accounts, and open new ones in individual names (open individual accounts before closing joint accounts, as credit may be easier to obtain that way).

- Split what's left and start over with a clean slate

	Linda	Joint	Tom	
House		$150,000		
Mortgage debt		($125,000)		
½ Net Equity	$12,500	-------	$12,500	½ Net Equity
½ Investments	$50,000	$100,000	$50,000	½ Investments
His 401k	$37,500	$75,000	$37,500	His 401k
Her car	$10,000	$30,000	$20,000	His car
Her car loan	($10,000)	($30,000)	($20,000)	His car loan
½ Credit card debt	($25,000)	($50,000)	($25,000)	½ Credit card debt
Net to wife	**$75,000**	**$150,000**	**$75,000**	**Net to husband**

Same net split; far different outcome. This would have truly severed the financial ties and taken the pressure off both parties to allow them to begin anew with a fresh start.

CASE STUDY 6: CAROLE BRODY FLEET

Carole Brody Fleet, Author / Founder
Widows Wear Stilettos
25422 Trabuco Road, Suite 105-148
Lake Forest, California 92630
www.widowswearstilettos.com
Carole@widowswearstilettos.com

No matter how perfect your life seems at any moment in time, bad things don't just happen to other people.

After caring for my husband through his battle with amyotrophic lateral sclerosis (ALS, or what is more commonly known as Lou Gehrig's Disease), I became a widow at the age of 40. This was a journey that culminated in physical and emotional shambles for my daughter and I, and was a complete

CASE STUDY 6: CAROLE BRODY FLEET

financial ruin. Like millions of other women who have experienced the loss of a spouse, I was left with a young daughter to raise (now 20), a mountain of bills to pay, a business to run, and absolutely no direction or instruction on how to accomplish any of it. Worse still, I could find no one to talk to who truly understood my situation. My friends and colleagues were either happily married and raising families or single by choice. Imagine, then, how it feels to have people physically back away from you when you tell them you are widowed (and apparently contagious), or to have to endure the insensitive opinions and observations of those around you, or try to figure out how the bills are going to be paid. How about figuring out how to raise young children who are themselves grieving; what the banks and creditors need for changes on accounts, mortgages, titles, and credit cards; the pros and pitfalls of re-entering the world of dating… and so much more.

After years had passed, and after having sufficiently recovered in all respects from what can only be described as the journey of a lifetime, I then decided:

If you can't find it, you create it.

The glaring lack of education and support for younger widows in particular, as well as a desire to ease others' pain, enhance lives, and coach widows of all ages, were the motivations leading to the inception of Widows Wear Stilettos in its entirety. It is incredibly rewarding to be able to educate, speak to, coach, and enrich women in need on a global level. It feels rewarding to help widows everywhere find comfort, solace, and community with other women in a most uncommon situation, using both necessary practical advice as well as a little bit of humor. when appropriate. Yes — there is a "lighter side" of widowhood).

In addition to the many thousands of visitors to the Web site and the hundreds of posts received on the message boards, I personally receive between 800 and 1,000 letters per week from widows all over the world. They ask questions, share stories, and express delight and relief at finding a community of compassion and understanding. They also find the education and resources that have been unfortunately lacking. Although Widows Wear Stilettos targets issues that primarily concern those who are widowed at a younger chronological age, we are thrilled to have members ranging in age from 17 to 88. It is vital that the messages of "what now and what next," as well as the support and encouragement of the thousands of women involved with Widows Wear Stilettos, continue to reach the millions of women who are so badly in need.

CASE STUDY 6: CAROLE BRODY FLEET

Widowhood changed me as a woman. Widows Wear Stilettos has forever transformed me as a person. It is both my privilege and my primary goal to help anyone who has suffered devastating loss, tragedy, or a serious life challenge on their respective healing journeys. It is also my goal to teach as many as possible that there is life after loss of any kind, and while this is perhaps not  the life you might have originally anticipated, it is nonetheless a life that you are entitled to lead in happiness, in abundance, and most importantly... in peace.

APPENDIX B:

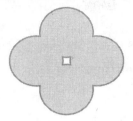

State Higher Education Agencies

- **Alabama**
  Alabama Commission on Higher Education
  www.ache.state.al.us

- **Alaska**
  Alaska Commission on Postsecondary Education
  http://alaskadvantage.state.ak.us

- **Arizona**
  Arizona Commission for Postsecondary Education
  www.azhighered.org

- **Arkansas**
  Arkansas Department of Higher Education
  www.arkansashighered.com

- **California**
  California Student Aid Commission
  www.csac.ca.gov

- **Colorado**
  Colorado Commission on Higher Education
  www.state.co.us/cche

- **Connecticut**
  Connecticut Department of Higher Education
  www.ctdhe.org

- **Delaware**
  Delaware Higher Education Commission
  www.doe.state.de.us/high-ed

- **District of Columbia**
  State Education Office (District of Columbia)
  www.seo.dc.gov

- **Florida**
  Office of Student Financial Assistance
  Florida Department of Education
  www.floridastudentfinancialaid.org

- **Georgia**
  Georgia Student Finance Commission
  www.gsfc.org

- **Hawaii**
  Hawaii Department of Education
  www.doe.k12.hi.us

- **Idaho**
  Idaho State Board of Education
  www.boardofed.idaho.gov

- **Illinois**
  Illinois Student Assistance Commission
  www.collegezone.com

- **Indiana**
  State Student Assistance Commission of Indiana
  www.ssaci.in.gov

- **Iowa**
  Iowa College Student Aid Commission
  www.iowacollegeaid.org

- **Kansas**
  Kansas Board of Regents
  www.kansasregents.org

- **Kentucky**
  Kentucky Higher Education Assistance Authority
  www.kheaa.com

- **Louisiana**
  Louisiana Office of Student Financial Assistance
  www.osfa.state.la.us

- **Maine**
  Finance Authority of Maine
  www.famemaine.com

- **Maryland**
  Maryland Higher Education Commission
  www.mhec.state.md.us

- **Massachusetts**
  Massachusetts Board of Higher Education
  www.osfa.mass.edu

- **Michigan**
  Michigan Higher Education Assistance Authority
  www.michigan.gov/mistudentaid

- **Minnesota**
  Minnesota Office of Higher Education
  www.ohe.state.mn.us

- **Mississippi**
  Mississippi office of Student Financial Aid
  www.ihl.state.ms.us

- **Missouri**
  Missouri Department of Higher Education
  www.dhe.mo.gov

- **Montana**
  Office of the Commissioner of Higher Education
  www.mus.edu/che/che.asp

- **Nebraska**
  Nebraska Coordinating Commission for Postsecondary Education
  www.ccpe.state.ne.us

- **Nevada**
  Nevada Department of Education
  www.doe.nv.gov

- **New Hampshire**
  New Hampshire Postsecondary Education Commission
  www.state.nh.us/postsecondary

- **New Jersey**
  Commission of Higher Education (New Jersey)
  www.state.nj.us/highereducation
  Higher Education Student Assistance Authority of New Jersey
  www.hesaa.org

- **New Mexico**
  New Mexico Higher Education Department
  www.hed.state.nm.us

- **New York**
  New York State Higher Education Services Corporation
  www.hesc.org

- **North Carolina**
  North Carolina State Education Assistance Authority
  www.cfnc.org

- **North Dakota**
  North Dakota University System
  www.ndus.edu

- **Ohio**
  Ohio Board of Regents
  http://regents.ohio.gov/

- **Oklahoma**
  Oklahoma State Regents for Higher Education
  www.okhighered.org

- **Oregon**
  Oregon Student Assistance Commission
  www.osac.state.or.us

- **Pennsylvania**
  Office of Postsecondary and Higher Education
  (Pennsylvania)
  www.pdehighered.state.pa.us

- **Rhode Island**
  Rhode Island Higher Education Assistance Authority
  www.riheaa.org

- **South Carolina**
  South Carolina Commission on Higher Education
  www.che400.state.sc.us

- **South Dakota**
  South Dakota Board of Regents
  www.sdbor.edu

- **Tennessee**
  Tennessee Student Assistance Corporation
  www.state.tn.us/tsac

- **Texas**
  Texas Higher Education Coordinating Board
  www.collegefortexans.com

- **Utah**
  Utah State Board of Regents
  www.utahsbr.edu

- **Vermont**
  Vermont Student Assistance Corporation
  www.vsac.org

- **Virginia**
  State Council of Higher Education for Virginia
  www.schev.edu

- **Washington**
  Washington State Higher Education Coordinating Board
  www.hecb.wa.gov

- **West Virginia**
  West Virginia Higher Education Policy Commission
  www.hepc.wvnet.edu

- **Wisconsin**
  Wisconsin Higher Educational Aids Board
  www.heab.state.wi.us

- **Wyoming**
  Wyoming Department of Education
  www.k12.wy.us

APPENDIX C:

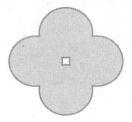

Resource Index

Bereavement Sources

- The Grief Recovery Institute: **www.grief.net**
- National Self-Help Clearinghouse: **http://mhselfhelp.org**
- Grief Help: **www.griefhelp.org**
- Help Guide: **www.helpguide.org**
- Journey of Hearts: **www.journeyofhearts.org**
- Child Grief: **www.childgrief.org**
- Mental Health Help: **www.mentalhealth.net**
- Funeral and Memorial Societies of America: **www.funerals.org**
- National Funeral Directors Associations: **www.NFDA.org**

Government Help

- Social Security Administration: **www.SSA.gov**
- Internal Revenue Service: **www.IRS.gov**
- Gift of Life Donation Initiative: **www.organdonor.gov**
- Department of Veterans Affairs: **www.va.gov**

- Federal Trade Commission's ID Theft Hotline: **www.consumer.gov/idtheft**

Career Help

- Dress for Success: **www.DressforSuccess.org**
- Career Gear: **www.careergear.org**
- Career Key: **www.careerkey.org**
- Job Seekers Advice: **www.jobseekersadvice.com**

Legal Help

- American Bar Association: **www.abanet.org**
- The American Academy of Matrimonial Lawyers: **www.aaml.org**

Insurance Help

- Fraud Insurance: **www.identityfraud.com**
- Health Insurance Information: **www.healthinsuranceinfo.net**
- Insurance Information Institute: **www.iii.org**
- Insure Kids Now: **www.insurekidsnow.gov**
- Medicare: **www.cms.hhs.gov**

Financial Help

- American College of Trust and Estate Counsel: **www.actec.org**
- American Association of Individual Investors: **www.aaii.com**
- Smart Money: **www.smartmoney.com**
- National Association of Financial Advisors: **www.napfa.org**

- Credit Information Center: **www.creditinfocenter.com**
- Credit Repair: **www.ftc.gov**
- Credit Consolidation: **www.consolidatedcredit.org**

Divorce Help

- Clearinghouse on Pensions and Divorce: (202) 296-3776
- Joint Custody Association: (310) 475-5352
- Divorce Helpline: **www.divorcehelp.com**
- DivorceNet: **www.divorcenet.com**
- Divorce Online: **www.divorceonline.com**
- Flying Solo: **www.flyingsolo.com**

Miscellaneous Help

- American Association of Retired Persons: **www.aarp.org**

BIBLIOGRAPHY

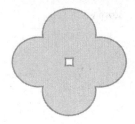

Garrett, Sheryl. <u>Surviving Divorce.</u> Chicago, Illinois: Dearborn Trade Publishing, 2006.

Garrett, Sheryl. <u>Surviving the Loss of a Spouse.</u> Chicago, Illinois: Dearborn Trade Publishing, 2006.

Ventura, John and Reed, Mary. <u>Divorce for Dummies.</u> Hoboken, New Jersey: Wiley Publishing Inc., 2005.

Woodhouse, Violet and Fetherling, Dale. <u>Divorce and Money: How to Make the Best Financial Decisions During Divorce.</u> Berkeley, California: NOLO Publishing, 2006.

Crouch, Holmes F. <u>Divorce & Its Tax Impact.</u> Saratoga, California: All Year Tax Guides Publishing Inc., 2006.

Baradihi, Fadi and Kurn, Nancy and Shepherd, Diana. <u>The IDFA Divorce Survival Guide.</u> Southfield, Michigan: The Institute of Divorce Financial Analysts, 2006.

Card, Emily and Kelly Watts, Christie. The Single Parent's Money Guide: A Blueprint for Managing Your Money When You're the Only One Your Family Can Count On. New York, New York: Macamillan Publishing USA, 1996.

Colgan, Mark R. The Survivor Assistance Handbook: A Guide for Financial Transition. Pitsford, New York: Plan Your Legacy LLC, 2007.

Connelly, Meg. 101 Things To Do The First Year of Your Divorce. Bloomington, Indiana: Author House Publishing, 2006.

Rogers, Brandon. 10 Things You Gotta Know About Paying for College. New York, New York: Spark Publishing, 2005.

Chany, Kalman A. and Martz, Geoff. Paying for College Without Going Broke 2008 Edition. New York, New York: Random House Publishing, 2007.

Tanabe, Gen and Kelly. How to Pay for College: A Practical Guide for Families. Los Altos, California: Supercollege LLC, 2005.

Ginsberg Davis Genevieve. Widow to Widow: Thoughtful and Practical Ideas for Rebuilding Your Life. Los Angeles, California: J.P. Tarcher, 1997.

Felber, Marta. Finding Your Way When Your Spouse Dies. Notre Dame, Indiana: Ave Maria Press, 2000.

Pat Nowak. The ABC's of Widowhood. Bloomington, Indiana: Pat Nowak, 2003.

Hallman, Victor G. and Rosenbloom, Jerry S. Personal Financial Planning. New York, New York: McGraw-Hill Publishing, 2003.

Clifford, Dennis. Estate Planning Basics. Berkeley, California: NOLO Publishing, 2006.

Palermo, Michael. The AARP Crash Course in Estate Planning: The Essential Guide to Wills, Trusts, and Your Personal Legacy. Washington, D.C.: AARP Publishing, 2007.

O'Donnell, Anne and Ingram, Peggy. My Money Myself: Hands-on Financial Planning Basics for Women of All Ages. Harrisonburg, Virginia: Choice Books, 2002.

Lawrence, Judy. The Budget Kit: The Common Cents Money Management Workbook. New York, New York: Kaplan Publishing 2008.

Dreuth, Tere. The Everything Budget Book. Avon, Massachusetts: Adams Media Corporation, 2003.

Woodward, Jeanette. Finding a Job After 50: Reinventing Yourself for the 21st Century. Franklin Lakes, New Jersey: Career Press, 2007.

Beshara, Tony. Job Search Solution: The Ultimate System to Finding a Great Job Now! New York, New York: AMACOM Publishing, 2006.

AUTHOR BIOGRAPHY

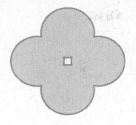

Maurcia DeLean Houck is a nationally known writer and editor with more than 1,500 bylines in 250 such well-known publications as *First for Women*, *Family Life*, *Writer's Digest*, *Your Health*, *AAA Going Places*, and *Modern Woman*.

She began her freelance career in 1991 while still serving as the executive editor of a mid-sized weekly newspaper in Philadelphia. She has also worked as a staff writer at several suburban newspapers in and around the Philadelphia area.

Houck is a 1999-2000 and 2000-2001 Inductee in Who's Who in the East and a former member of the National Writer's Association (1994-1999).

INDEX

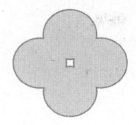

U

V

W